You Are a F*cking Success

ABOUT THE AUTHOR

Noor Hibbert is the *Sunday Times* bestselling author of *Just F*cking Do it* and *You Only Live Once*. She is a transformation coach, serial entrepreneur and runs workshops on how to transform your mindset so you can master manifestation and create your dream life.

You Are a F*cking Success

Change Your Story, Manifest Your Dream Life

NOOR HIBBERT

BUSINESS

PENGUIN BUSINESS

UK | USA | Canada | Ireland | Australia
India | New Zealand | South Africa

Penguin Business is part of the Penguin Random House group of companies
whose addresses can be found at global.penguinrandomhouse.com.

First published 2024
001

Set in 11.28/13.86pt Dante MT Std
Typeset by Jouve (UK), Milton Keynes
Printed and bound in Great Britain by Clays Ltd, Elcograf S.p.A.

The authorized representative in the EEA is Penguin Random House Ireland,
Morrison Chambers, 32 Nassau Street, Dublin D02 YH68

A CIP catalogue record for this book is available from the British Library

ISBN: 978-0-241-62941-3

www.greenpenguin.co.uk

MIX
Paper | Supporting
responsible forestry
FSC® C018179

Penguin Random House is committed to a
sustainable future for our business, our readers
and our planet. This book is made from Forest
Stewardship Council® certified paper.

To my four incredible children: Layla-Rose,
Safia-Lily, Amira-Jasmine and Caspar. You are my
greatest achievement, and my biggest intention is that
you create a life better than your wildest dreams.

I love you with every cell in my body. Thank you for
choosing me to be your mummy. It has been
the greatest journey of my life.

Contents

Contents

PART ONE
The Meaning

Success: We got it all f*cking wrong

'Gucci, Chanel, Mulberry! Come and get your handbags – cheaper than Asda, cheaper than Tesco!'

I giggled as I walked down the colourful streets in Turkey, lined with stalls selling everything you could possibly imagine. The heat of the Mediterranean sun warmed my sixteen-year-old skin as I took in the hustle and bustle of the market-sellers eagerly enticing holidaymakers into their tiny space, shouting over each other, coercing them to purchase knock-off handbags, watches and trainers that were supposedly cheaper than those in the supermarkets back in the UK.

I was so excited: I'd finally be able to buy myself a designer handbag. 'No one would know it was a fake,' I told myself convincingly.

I desperately wanted to know what it felt like to be able to walk around proudly with a Gucci clutch, or one of those little padded Chanel bags that look like they are made from a quilt. Because those things are symbols of success, right? Only 'successful' people, or those with rich parents, could afford expensive make-up, designer handbags, fast cars and mansions. They might be douchebags, but who cares? They were successful and they must be happy. And I wanted some of that!

I deeply hated the feeling I got whenever I was around people who had nice things that I couldn't afford. Things that I truly believed I'd *never* be able to afford – certainly not as a teenager or in my twenties. Things that I believed would somehow make me a happier and better person. This is the story our ego tells us.

Our ego – the part of us that we create during our human existence – sucks us in and when we follow its lead, believing that its voice and desires are *our* true voice and desires, we are misled into the false promise that success is somehow marked by the items we own, or that this type of success is inextricably linked with our happiness during our lifetime. Why? Because we live in a society with a huge focus on materialism and attachment.

After my purchase of said knock-off handbag, I immediately felt my first leather-induced dopamine rush. This is the temporary high that comes when you momentarily satiate your ego's desires. One of the driving goals of the ego is 'to get'. So once that first high wears off, we start scrambling around the streets like a drug addict, trying to find the next thing that will make us *feel* successful, important, happy, wealthy or worthy; the next fix to enable us to escape mediocrity – always looking outside ourselves for an answer. Whether it is found in handbags, fame or social-media 'likes', we unconsciously hunt for this feeling, believing it will make us feel fulfilled.

But what if, as humans, we have got things completely f*cking wrong? What if we have all bought into the terrifying delusion that we cannot be happy if we aren't 'successful', because we have a warped meaning of the word – a meaning based on what we have been taught by society? What if our meaning of success has been so distorted, like a game of Chinese whispers, and we've been sold the idea it's a destination that seems to be on the other side of the world and we have no roadmap or transport to get there safely or quickly? If we roamed the streets and asked people what success meant, you might hear some of the comments below:

- Success is a certain level of educational attainment.
- Success is a particular career, like becoming a doctor or lawyer [or insert any other profession that makes you sound super-clever].
- Success is limited to the lucky few and is not something that can be achieved by all.
- Success is fame.
- Success is measured by your wealth.

- Success is wearing designer clothes, driving fast cars and owning mansions.
- Success is looking like a Kardashian.
- Success is marrying a rich man.
- Success only happens to those with a particular personality trait.
- Success means being better than everyone else.
- Success is a fancy car, a big house and 2.4 children, who are so well behaved and refer to you as Mumsy and Papa; they never have a tantrum in public, always have their hair neatly brushed and know never to leave the table until dinner is finished.

You see, the mainstream story we get spoon-fed is that success is something to be attained: a destination to arrive at and a place where we will somehow be complete, once we get there. As I began the most important journey of my life – the journey of understanding who I was, why I was here and what I was really capable of – the first thing I began to wake up to was the fact that we were mis-sold what success is by a world driven by capitalism, consumerism and Botox, leaving us disconnected from our true purpose and from a deeper meaning of what being successful truly means. We believe that success is marked by the things we attain *outside* us. This leaves us consistently feeling like we are in lack and disconnected. Consequently we begin looking for things to fill us up in the external world, searching for some sort of connection in the wrong places and scrambling for the roadmap to this elusive destination.

Therefore life often feels like you are turning one page at a time, hoping that somehow you will reach the plot twist where everything works out better, but sometimes that page never seems to come. The problem with this way of life is that we don't ever truly enjoy the journey, and most of us are never satisfied if we do arrive where we have striven to get to. That is because, with every success that we achieve, there is only a small window of time before we move on to the next goal and the next desire, because the ego never really feels done. Like a balloon that has a hole so small it's hard to see, even if we keep filling it with air (or material things, in this case), the ego will slowly deflate. No matter how much we exhaust our lungs blowing it up or how many times we try to fill it up again, we wonder in confusion why it keeps getting smaller; we know that somehow the air is escaping, yet are unable to locate the penetrating hole. I believe this hole represents a void inside us, because fundamentally, as humans, we see success through a materialistic and individualistic lens.

Our whole life is determined by the meanings that we give things. They are the stories we have built up in our minds about pretty much everything in life. They are the stories that we have about what 'success' is, and these stories create the book of our lives. Sometimes that book is good, sometimes the book is bad and on occasions the book is really f*cking ugly.

Having worked with thousands of people across the globe, it's clear to me that overall these stories are not conducive to feeling happy and fulfilled. As someone who felt such lack and disconnection for most of my life, it's almost impossible not to reverse-engineer my story, or the lives of my clients, to see what happened.

After some deep observation, I believe that we have an overwhelming number of people feeling stuck, lost and sad because, at a basic level, we spend our lives chasing this elusive white rabbit that represents a skewed version of success, instead of looking for true connection, meaning and fulfilment. Subsequently, by the time we find out the rabbit wasn't actually white or fluffy at all, we are in debt. Companies thrive on preying on our weaknesses, persuading us each day that somehow we aren't good enough just as we are. They make money out of us when we are driven by our egos' needs, and the worst part is that we don't even know it's happening. And then came social media . . . and everybody was fucked.

Social media has become an addiction for many. It gives us a chance to showcase our lives for 'likes', so that our ego gets that fix from feeling important. But it also means that we now have millions of people to compare ourselves to, which heightens any internal belief that we aren't good enough. Social media portrays and perpetrates a version of success that leaves most people feeling spiritually bankrupt, because maybe we do feel happy, but then we find ourselves scrolling on Instagram and suddenly the external comparisons convince us that we are not. And then . . . *boom*! We get lured in by the next advert we see on our newsfeed.

'You will feel so f*cking important, like all those celebrities, if you buy me,' the handbag whispers.

'You will feel better than everyone else if you own me,' the watch mutters gently.

'You will feel wealthy and worthy when you drive me,' shouts the luxury car that you can't afford.

And before you know it, the credit card is whipped out and another expensive purchase is made – all in the name of making you feel temporarily better. However, once we run out of real (or fake) handbags to buy, the danger is that we move on to other things, such as alcohol, sex, drugs and relationships, to make us feel better.

Let me make one thing clear: there is nothing wrong with buying fancy things and owning nice stuff, and there is nothing wrong with spending your hard-earned money on material items that you desire. In fact, doing things that make us feel good is surely the purpose of life. However, the problem arises when you buy stuff you cannot afford or don't really want, but are driven by the belief that it will fill a void, or that you will be perceived in a certain way. This is trickery by the ego guiding your decisions because of an unconscious fear of not being good enough.

Changing the story

That's why we absolutely need to change the story – and pretty freaking *pronto*. What if our new story is that being successful isn't about becoming anything or anyone different, or even about getting anywhere, but is about *un*becoming everything we have become, so that we can remember that *we are already a f*cking success*? Yes, the fact that you were born as *you* – which is a 1-in-400 trillion chance – means that you were a success from the moment you exited your mother's womb.

You see, we all desire to live *la dolce vita*: a life that tastes as sweet as your favourite ice cream, with a melt-in-your-mouth bar of chocolate popped inside. However, the reality is that most of us live our *vita* with the sweet part somehow left out.

That's why I felt it was so important to write this book, to support you in figuring out what flavour of life you want, and not only to help you get there, but to show you how to do it with an abundance of multicoloured sprinkles on top. I don't know who you are (yes, you: the one who is reading this), but thank you from the bottom of my heart for taking the time to be on this journey. Thank you for investing your most valuable asset – your attention – and I fully intend to give you an ROI (return on investment). I want us to begin with the intention that we need to collectively change the conversation around success so that every single one of us has the opportunity to bask in the deliciousness of what it means to feel true abundance and peace in our lives. I feel that now, more than ever, humans are asking, 'Is this it?' and desiring more connection, meaning and fulfilment. And the way to do that is by *changing the story of what success means for us.*

We need to stop measuring our place in this world by the attainment of material objects. We need to stop the narrative that success is measured by our net-worth and social-media likes, otherwise we end up like that balloon, on a constant downward spiral to deflation. We need to stop looking for success outside ourselves and seek to look inwards for what we truly desire, because we are seeing catastrophic consequences: mental-health issues are rising by the day, physical problems are becoming more chronic, and studies have shown that more and more people lack purpose and fulfilment in their lives. We have a responsibility to each other to shift this, so that we can all collectively feel happier, with a sense of purpose.

When we don't understand what our purpose is during our lives, how will we ever achieve real contentment and thus success? When we believe that we aren't successful (because we don't have our own definition of this word) and we don't know how to create this supposed success, an energetic wound appears, caused by the internal discomfort – just like that hole in the balloon.

As a result, we will do anything to stop the wound being exposed and to alleviate the sting of an unfulfilled life, and the belief that somehow we aren't good enough or perfect, exactly as we are. But instead of healing the wound, most of us unconsciously seek to fill it with things to make us feel better. Sadly, many people then negatively attempt to find solace in alcohol, drugs, sex and social-media likes, because as humans we aren't taught a framework for how to live our lives in a more positive way.

We all want to feel important and that our lives have meaning. I want to help you truly look at yourself and your life, because full-bodied awareness is the only way to create true transformation and a life with deep meaning. I want to provide a framework in this book for deep change, because, as humans, we have a fundamental desire to grow and self-actualize.

That is probably why you picked this book up, because at some level you want to have, do or be more. More *what*? I don't know, because I don't know you personally. But my suspicion is that wherever you are in life right now doesn't feel as happy or as abundant as where you could be, or where you desire to be. Or maybe you have reached a certain level of success, but don't feel it in your soul and you feel duped or confused. There is nothing wrong with wanting more. There is nothing wrong with striving to be the best version of yourself, working your way up the career ladder, bettering yourself educationally and financially, because as humans we are here to grow. It's the intentions behind every action that are paramount. We need to stop and ask ourselves *why* we are doing what we are doing, rather than pushing every day with no real awareness of what we are pushing for.

We all have so much untapped potential, yet for the most part we are unconscious of how we are behaving, and we become constantly distracted from the bigger picture of who we are and why we are here. This is not our fault, and we will delve further into the power of the subconscious mind later on.

When we operate with an outside-in approach to life, we are seeking to fill gaps; and the type of gap that we are trying to fill will never be satisfactorily filled with material items or things outside ourselves. Why? Because we are spiritual beings with a soul, and our soul desires more than a f*cking handbag. As we are spiritual beings, we aspire to reach our full potential, but we get stuck along the way because no one gave us the roadmap to real happiness. As someone who has felt the pain that feeling 'not good enough' can bring, and the sting of feeling 'less than' others, I can tell you that I unconsciously sought to fill my voids with alcohol, drugs and relationships, instead of going inwards to try and heal my wounds.

The reality is that we can see proof daily that external success does not make for deeply happy people. All we have to do is take a look at the media headlines concerning yet another seemingly super-successful A-list celebrity who has checked into rehab. 'But why?' you might ask. How do they have the audacity to feel they are suffering? They've got everything they could ever want: money, fame, success? What could possibly be wrong with them! They are so successful. But just as my 'designer' knock-off handbag began to fray, the straps started to break and the logo on it began to fade, so 'cheap' success doesn't last long. When I say 'cheap' success, what I mean is the success that we are taught to believe is success. The success that many celebrities create, and that social media portrays.

Humanoids

In my last book, *You Only Live Once*, I explained that one of the things I realized was holding us back from creating abundance was that many of us humans are running on autopilot and are unconscious as to why we are living life as we are.

I refer to this as 'humanoid behaviour'. Humanoids are normal everyday people, who operate from the belief system that we are here to eat, sleep, work, repeat, save for a pension and die. And if we are lucky, we'll sneak in a cheeky Caribbean cruise along the way. I know this well, because 'I am Noor and I am a recovering humanoid.'

I went from job to job for a decade, trying to make money. I worked on everything from being a promo girl for Red Bull, to credit-card sales at football matches, to standing at a stall in supermarkets trying to get people to sign up for health insurance. I've worked on a make-up counter in Debenhams, for a video-games training company, at an after-school club looking after children and as a Club 18–30 holiday rep. I've been a gym-membership consultant, a nightclub promoter and a nursery nurse. I was finding any way to survive and make money.

This 'survival' operating mode means that often humanoids don't do anything fulfilling, and don't live a life that is driven by purpose or guided by their unique blueprint for creating abundance and feeling they are creating success. I don't think humans are just plonked here on planet Earth with no purpose except to figure out 'how to survive'. I happen to believe that each of us has a unique blueprint, within which lies our purpose on this planet and how we can contribute to humankind. Life is a bit like an orienteering exercise and we simply need to use an inner compass that points to our true north – our own version of success and our most abundant life. That's why I truly believe that purpose and success are inextricably linked.

When someone is living a life that is lacking in purpose, they never feel fulfilled, even if they have money to buy the items they want, because they aren't doing what they want to or are meant to be doing. They are unconsciously driven by their basic survival needs, such as shelter and food. No one creates a successful life when living *only* in survival mode. Even if they are able to create more money and abundance, they won't feel the sweetness of it, because the way they got there was stressful or through hard work, and wasn't in alignment with their purpose and their unique blueprint.

Living with purpose

Success, I've come to learn, is very much a *conscious* choice, not an unconscious reaction to life. *Living a life on purpose, and with purpose, is a prerequisite to being successful*:

- Success is a feeling that is cultivated when things are good.
- Success is about how you choose to feel, in the absence of material things.
- Success is about finding the path in life that lights you up and gives your life meaning, so that you can wake up every day feeling grateful for being here, not resentful of the day ahead.
- Success is choosing to be the best version of yourself every day.

The only yardstick of success should be the one you create for yourself; it is not a measure against others. So the first step is awareness, and a conscious effort to stop living through the narrative that we are helpless and powerless to transform our reality. We need to start to understand where our stories have come from and how to rewrite them for a brighter future, with each page filled with captivating tales of the way we became the hero or heroine of our own life, not the victim of our circumstances.

Living life inside-out

If you don't like how your life is shaping up, then it's probably a good time to decide to change it. And that's exactly what I want to do with you in this book, starting with what success *really* means. So I'm about to throw out a crazy idea – a revolutionary idea, an idea that literally tipped my life on its head and caused my physical reality to shift in front of my very eyes.

What if success isn't defined by the things I can get / buy / attain?

What if I can feel successful, happy and fulfilled without all that stuff? What if I don't rely on purchases to make me feel peace and joy? What if I can find out what my true purpose is, so that I can create incredible abundance that feels good, instead of simply surviving?

My sincere intention, as I wrote this book, was to help you redefine the meaning of success and support you in re-creating the story of your own reality, by connecting you to what truly matters to *you*. This in turn will make you more successful than you ever imagined possible. The truth is that only one person can change your life – and that person is *you*.

A mentor once told me that if I could *feel* successful first, then I could create a life better than my wildest dreams and manifest all the abundance I desired. And so that's exactly what I did. I slowly began to live my life from an inside-out approach. I became obsessed with how to develop myself personally and started to accept a new way of thinking. When I talk about 'manifesting', I simply mean the physical realization of something that is a desire – a thought snuggled in the confines of my own mind.

It was not an overnight journey by any means, but I went from crying on my knees in my living room, heartbroken that my life was falling apart in front of my eyes, to seeing the craziest dreams come to fruition, as though some wizardry was occurring. I went from living on £138-a-week maternity benefits and no clue what I was going to do, to creating a business that I love, while fuelling my desire for freedom and not having to live life by the rules that society told me to. I then created an income beyond my wildest dreams. Success isn't about money; money is the fuel for doing the things I love most and for being able to give to those I care about. One of my biggest lessons from the last decade is that my level of success is directly proportional to how much I am willing to expand as a person, from the inside out. I cannot wait to delve into this in more detail with you.

In the first part of the book we are looking into the meaning of success, your unique purpose and how you have come to believe the things you do about money; and we will examine the inner workings of the mind, so that you can see why you are the person you are today. I want to share perspectives that will give you multiple 'Aha' moments and enable you to break through to the next level in your life.

I created success on my own terms, and that success was defined by me, not anyone else. And guess what? I never once looked at buying a designer handbag again. And I'm so excited, Dear Reader (that sounds very *Bridgerton*), to help you do the same. I want to help you crack open every belief you have about life and your ability to change it, and my aspiration is that you shatter every glass ceiling that your thoughts were limiting. I know it's a bold aspiration, but I'm willing to take on the task. If that sounds like a fun journey to go on, then keep reading, because we are about to change your story so that you manifest your dream life.

2.

Ordinary people, extraordinary lives

You're already a few pages into this book and it's kinda rude of me that I haven't properly introduced myself. The book cover clearly says my name, but who am I? Well, first and foremost I'm the mummy to four pretty incredible small humans.

Second, I'm a qualified coach, with a degree in psychology and postgraduate certificates in both business and executive coaching and in coaching psychology. I've trained with some of the best people in the world in many other modalities to strengthen my craft as a coach, and I'm the creator of the VIA Manifesting Method® (see page 57) and the author of two bestselling books. I'm also obsessed with understanding how to help people become the happiest version of themselves by harnessing the power of their subconscious mind and by utilizing Subconscious Rescripting® (see page 89). I have the heart of a hippie, the mouth of a sailor and, if I had a choice, I'd live in tracksuits.

I am deeply passionate about helping people to transform their lives because, if I'm brutally honest, there was a point in my life as a teenager when I was on my bed, drinking a bottle of Malibu and contemplating the best way to end it all. Life was hard. I'd been through a series of traumatic life events, and by the time I was sixteen I was diagnosed with depression. I remember very specifically this time in my life because I was battling with myself, on a daily basis, not to end it. I didn't think anybody would care. I remember saying to myself, 'If I were to die, it would be so much easier.' I was estranged from my dad, disconnected from my mum, and in a toxic relationship with a boy who was older than me, who emotionally blackmailed me to stay with him by attempting to commit suicide and blaming me.

By the time I was nineteen I had started taking medication to ease my anxiety, and throughout my twenties I was drinking myself into oblivion, sniffing questionable powders off toilet seats and going from one relationship to another, in the hope that I would somehow find myself, find love or find true happiness. If I wasn't stuck in thoughts of my past, I would be plagued with worries of the future – it was a mental prison that I felt powerless to escape.

It wasn't all doom and gloom, though, as I met some of my bestest friends in those years. I worked abroad in the sunny Mediterranean as a Club 18–30 rep and have many Jägerbomb-fuelled memories of booze cruises, foam parties and school discos. But behind my confident smile was a wounded girl who believed she was a victim of her life and her circumstances; a girl who had picked the short straw and was destined to have one bad thing happen after another. I never ever felt a sense of belonging or that I fitted in anywhere in life. That's a weird feeling to have, but I always felt like an outsider in any social group or setting.

What is most weird now, though, is that as the years pass and I get further and further away from that version of the girl, it becomes harder to write about her. I don't believe in dwelling on the past, but I think that – by establishing the context of who I am and where I have come from – I should enable you to see that I was not born lucky; I created my success on my own terms and was not handed it by anyone.

In 2015 something shifted inside me while I was dealing with one of the most difficult periods of my life. I was curled up in a ball on my living-room floor, my face was soaked with tears, my mind racing. *Who was I? How was this my life? Why was this happening to me?* I realized that I simply responded to life. Whatever life threw at me, I just responded and it felt like there was nothing I could do about it, nor did I believe that I had any control over what was happening. I had relinquished all responsibility when I made the decision that I was a depressed and anxious person who was doomed to have unlucky things continually happening. I felt I had no power and that life was just going to happen to me forever.

It was a dark moment in my life, but for the sake of my beautiful daughters I made a decision deep within my soul to change and to take back my power. I would no longer be a victim; no longer would I allow fear to run the show; and no longer would I settle for anything other than what I truly wanted. I didn't want to be simply a response to my world, because that meant when life was good, I was good; and when life was bad, I was really bad. I wanted to make my life f*cking great. In that dark night of my soul, something profound happened – I started to move towards the light. I realized I wanted so much more than this.

Let me continue by saying that I am not from a wealthy background, and I didn't have anyone in my family who was a millionaire. We were normal people, and my parents – who had moved from the Middle East in their teenage years – both worked incredibly hard to give us a decent life. My parents had me very young, and I can assure you that was less from choice and more because no one had taught them about contraception! As a child, I watched my mum endure long days and night-shifts as a young nurse, and my dad leaving for the London Tube in the early morning to go and fulfil his dream of becoming a solicitor. They both worked long hours and, while we never wanted for anything, it wasn't until I joined a private school in year five, at nine years old, that I began to understand what wealth was and how different my life was, compared to that of other children.

I knew I was different from the minute I joined Wimbledon High School – not only because I was one of the few browner kids, but because we seemed less well-off financially. Putting me into private education was a huge stretch for my parents, but one they strongly believed in; because both of them were Middle Eastern, they regarded education as a pivotal part of achieving 'success'.

While I used to proudly tell everyone that my mum was a care-home manager and my dad was a lawyer, our life didn't seem to mirror the success of others with those fancy titles. Instead of a huge house in an affluent part of Wimbledon, we lived in a tiny ex-council house on the outskirts. Instead of multiple holidays a year, skiing, sailing and heading to posh resorts in Portugal, we would be searching on Teletext for the cheapest holidays we could find.

My parents had to work so much that we had a live-in Spanish au pair looking after us for most of our childhoods, so that my parents could afford to pay for our school and for us to live. When I say 'au pair', people's ears prick up and suddenly imagine an expensive live-in nanny who wore an apron, like in *Peter Pan*. In reality, the au pairs who looked after us were usually girls who lived in the local convent, who were Spanish and in their very early twenties. They would move in with us, in our little box bedroom, in return for looking after us. They were very much part of my everyday life and did the majority share of bringing us up as children; they are one of the reasons I often get told, 'Noor, when you speak Spanish, your accent sounds incredible!' That was life for me; I saw my parents briefly each evening and at weekends and, because of their fraught relationship, my childhood memories are, sadly, not full of butterflies and unicorns.

The jump from state school to private education was huge for me. I always felt like an outsider and was distinctly average at everything. My parents were then forced to spend more money on getting me a tutor, so that I could reach the academic level of the other children, which made me feel like I was dumb, and guilty. I didn't really excel at anything, never made it onto the sports teams and was far from popular.

I'll never forget when a new girl joined the sixth form. As I was the outsider of all the cliques in the year, I loved it when someone new joined. The first time she invited me to her house, my stepdad drove me. She lived in Wimbledon Village and, when we got to her address, we couldn't even see where she lived. We were taken down a long, winding drive, lined with huge trees, that seemed to go on and on – it felt like I was in Narnia. At the end of the drive I caught sight of a building. 'This must be her house!' my stepdad said in disbelief. We both looked in amazement, wondering if we had come to the right place. As I glanced up, I saw turrets. Yes, turrets. My friend lived in a f*cking castle!

Her dad, I soon came to learn, was on the UK's Rich List and had sold his software business for multi-multimillions. *Wow!* This is what it was like to be wealthy. I wandered the halls of this castle home, which happened to have belonged to Henry VIII, trying to act cool, as though I frequented castles on a weekly basis.

Needless to say, I didn't believe I was one of the 'lucky' ones who could create that level of success or wealth, like my friend's family had. You needed to be super-smart to be successful and, to be honest, I'd never met a millionaire in my life until that day and felt like I was with celebrities. I wanted a big house, nice things and fancy holidays, but I didn't believe it was possible for people like me. I was just an ordinary person, and ordinary people didn't create extraordinary lives. But, as you will come to learn in this book, belief is the foundation for everything that we create in our lives.

When it came to job-hunting after university, I was completely happy to go for a £30,000-a-year job, because that's what everyone did, right? If you had said to me six years ago, 'Noor you will be a millionaire by thirty-five', I would have believed you more if you'd told me that Earth would be invaded by aliens. Considering that only a decade ago I was on £138-a-week maternity pay, feeling lost and confused about my purpose in life, and have now got to the point where I have a business that I adore and that has made more than £3 million, while I am also a full-time mummy to four humans, it's pretty mind-blowing to me.

Finding your own blueprint

On my humbling journey I've come to learn a few things about transforming life and creating success, and I cannot wait to drop the curtain and give you an in-depth view into what success really is, what it isn't and *how to actually create it*.

I've come to learn that being financially successful doesn't mean that you are happy. You can be the richest person in the world, yet you can be plagued by depression or anxiety. Money does not fix internal wounds or past trauma. Your net-worth does not equate to your self-worth, but your self-worth will absolutely correlate to your net-worth – we will talk about the importance of your relationship with money later on in the book (see Chapter 14).

Money can be the means to buy things that make you happy, but only if you truly understand what makes your soul happy – not what you *think* you should have in order to make you happy. You can use money as a vehicle to get those items and create those experiences, but it will only be a sticking plaster for the wound.

The means to gaining financial success needs to be in alignment with your unique blueprint and what is suited to you as a human, otherwise the fruits of your labour will always come with a sour taste and will be like my knock-off handbag: cheap and temporary. Here are a few things I've come to learn about success:

- Success is different for everyone, and until you clearly define what that looks like for you and why it's important, you will forever be chasing someone else's dream.
- Success is *not* defined by the things we have. I live in £10 leggings most of the time and in one of my many hoodies.
- Success is a feeling. Or a myriad of feelings. We want everything we want in life because of the *feeling* it will give us. *Read that again.* We need to understand what that feeling is for us. We chase that feeling, instead of realizing that we have the power to cultivate it whenever we want. We need to go inwards first.

We may be ordinary people, but each of us is a miracle. The fact that you are reading this book tells me one pretty important thing: you beat the 1-in-400 trillion chance of being born. And one last thing, which I know for sure: ordinary people are creating extraordinary lives, and I want you to be the next person to do so. We need to stop operating on autopilot and start to consciously create what we desire, and one of the easier ways to create abundance is by following our purpose. Each of us has a unique soul blueprint that unlocks our greatest, most successful life, so let's dive in.

3.

Mission 'not so' impossible

I was walking through the woods near my house and as autumn began to settle in, and I noticed the leaves that were beginning to shift from green to brown, I contemplated what my purpose on this planet was. As I allowed the cool air to enter my lungs, I noticed that the path in front was strewn with acorns. Acorns that would for ever remain acorns, until they rotted or got stomped on by strollers unknowingly walking by. Acorns that would never actualize into becoming a fully-fledged oak tree.

It got me thinking about us humans: we are all just little acorns waiting to reach our full potential of becoming an oak tree. You see, an acorn is destined to be an oak tree; it's written in the stars and that is its purpose. Coded within the seed is the blueprint to take it from acorn to oak. But for it to become an oak tree, it needs good soil, plenty of water and exactly the right amount of sunshine. And, most importantly, time and space to enable the seed to be nurtured and gestate, because a tree does not sprout overnight, but over time. Even though the fate of that acorn is to be an oak tree, if the environment for its success isn't there, the acorn can end up staying as that seed, diverted from reaching its full potential and on a path to being squished by a toddler jumping in the leaves, or gobbled down by a squirrel on an autumn day.

I believe we are all blueprinted for success. It's like we have an invincible microchip containing the vital data for what our best life could look like. I believe that each of us has a unique purpose and mission – something that gives our lives meaning, fulfilment and a way in which we can contribute to others while creating abundance for ourselves. And while you may not realize it just yet, fulfilling this mission will be *the* most important thing you will ever do in your lifetime. It's also the most important thing you can do in order to create the life of your dreams. Most of us never get to reach that fullest expression of ourselves because we are limited by our paradigms and get stuck in survival mode, thanks to our over-protective mind.

Let me illustrate this using a hypothetical story, based on a fictional set of scenarios. Once upon a time I walked into a supermarket and there was a cashier called Beyoncé Knowles. Her voice was nothing short of sensational and it was clear that her purpose on this planet was to make people feel a certain way through her music and her voice. She would spend hours as a little girl staring into the mirror, singing to imaginary audiences, dreaming vividly of becoming a global superstar touching the lives of millions through her music.

But Beyoncé was just a cashier. She didn't truly believe she was capable of creating success, because she had grown up in a family where everyone worked for the minimum wage. She let the voice in her head dissuade her from going to auditions. She let the murmur of society telling her to get a comfortable job steer her away from following that fate. Beyoncé stayed as cashier until she was fifty and then finally graduated to supermarket manager, but she never became a global superstar.

This could easily have happened, but – thank the Lord – Beyoncé Knowles didn't end up as a manager at Walmart. She took a different path, followed her dreams and became a global superstar. Why? Because she honoured her unique blueprint and followed her purpose. Now let's talk about *your unique blueprint.*

Living in accordance with your dharma

I'm sure you've come across the term 'microchipping'. It's the process whereby a computer chip is implanted under the skin of the family pet, so that it can be traced if it ever gets lost. This microchip contains the unique data for individual animals! Your unique blue-print is just like a tiny microchip implanted within you, containing spiritual information about who you are, why you're here and what you're meant to achieve in your lifetime. How do we know what our unique blueprint holds? Well, clues to our purpose, or dharma, are often found coded within our deepest desires and dreams.

The ancient Sanskrit word *dharma* refers to your soul's purpose, which is the big reason you are on Earth for your lifetime. But here's the important thing about your dharma: it's not simply what you do, but *how* you do it and *why* you do it. It's how you 'be', not what you do. Once again, this comes back to the fact that we are human *beings*, not human *doings*.

Your dharma is not a career, or a project, or a certain role you play. It's the unique vibration that your soul carries and how you apply that to everything you do and every way that you are. For instance, someone's dharma can be to bring beauty to the world, and how they achieve that can be in so many different ways, such as through being an artist, a landscape designer, a hairstylist or an architect. My dharma is to heal and help others, and I do that through my coaching, courses, books and podcasts. But the *way* I do it is the unique expression of me – sprinkled with swearing and finished off with a layer of typos, to keep it real.

Beyoncé contributes to the world through her incredible music and her gift for singing, and she has become very wealthy from doing so. That was her soul's purpose on this planet and she had the right soil, good sun and plenty of water to make that happen. Trans-lated into something you can better understand, she had her vision, identity and action locked in, so she set herself up for success.

However, just because we are given our dharma doesn't mean we will inevitably live it out. Even though it's written in the stars that we can create success, and we are given the machinery in our phys-ical body to create it, that does not mean it will happen. We are all destined for great things and to create the abundance we desire, but we need to manifest that into a reality.

Going back to the acorn, it needs soil for it to grow. The soil represents the field of pure potentiality, the energy field of the universe – the invisible stuff through which everything comes to physical manifestation. It is where all the potential outcomes of the world can be created, and is also how you reach your fullest potential. The more connected we are to this field, the easier it is to manifest what we desire. But connecting to it is a choice. The more disconnected from it we are, the more blocks and resistance we feel.

There are *three layers* to living a life full of meaning and fulfilment, so let's start by understanding these layers. First things first: if you believe you are only here to eat, sleep, work, save for your pension and die, then you are locked into survival mode. When I started to see myself as a spiritual being, connected to an infinite source of intelligence (call it the universe, God, mother nature, Allah, your higher self or whatever), I began to understand that I had a direct impact on my life. Rather than life happening *to* me, I started to appreciate that life happened as a *result* of me. This alone took me from accidentally living to consciously creating. I realized that I wasn't here by accident, that my soul had chosen to joyride in my physical body and that my overriding purpose was to create a life better than I could have ever dreamed of, through helping others do the same.

I wasn't going to be deeply happy and fulfilled if I did what I was told I 'should' do and didn't follow what I was *meant* to do. So many of us get stuck in this mentality of 'I should', because we feel this will keep us in line with societal expectations. However, I wasn't going to expand if I kept 'should-ing' all over my life, instead of doing what I *desired*. And I certainly wasn't going to be happy living in survival mode and on autopilot. That leads us to the *second layer*, which is that I needed to become aware of how I was showing up in my life and, instead of clock-watching my life away because of my boring job, that's why I chose to live *on purpose*.

I learned this concept from the late Jim Rohn, who was an American entrepreneur, author and motivational speaker, and a dead dude that I spent most of my time with while I was pregnant with my eldest daughter. I took a job in sales, because I needed the money.

While I drove countless miles across the country to visit potential clients, I became addicted to personal development. Something Jim said on one of the many audios that I devoured really hit home for me. He said that instead of showing up for a job that you hated like you hated it, the quickest way to get out of the job you hated was to start showing up like you loved it. He encouraged his listeners to embrace each and every day with joy, and to bring energy to that day as though it was your last day on this planet. He said that through this, things would start to change.

I had nothing to lose, so instead of dreading each day, I made a conscious effort to show up with a different attitude. What I came to understand later was that what Jim was teaching was 'vibrational alignment'. I was never going to create my dream life from a place of hating my own life. They were two completely different frequencies, and they were different realities on different wavelengths.

Once we have peeled back the first two layers, we reveal the *final layer*, which is uncovering our own unique purpose because we are tuned into the right frequency. Most people are trying to uncover their purpose while they are tuned into completely the wrong wavelength.

It's like switching the radio onto a sports channel and hoping you will get dance music. You can listen to that sports channel all day, waiting patiently for a dance track to come and feeling disappointed when you get stuck listening to men discussing the latest tackle or transfer. But if you press the arrow and watch as the radio tunes into a different wavelength, once those numbers stop rolling and you land on the right frequency for your favourite radio station, *boom!* – the music plays and you can do the Macarena all the way to Purpose-ville. You need to consciously change your frequency, tune into the right wavelength and you will be guided towards your dharma. You cannot create the next level of your life from the same level of thinking that got you here – certainly not while tuned into the wrong wavelength.

Once you start to live on purpose and you are dialled into another frequency, you will be able to see with more clarity than ever before what your purpose is (or your purposes are). Yes, you are allowed to have more than one purpose – shock, horror!

Life is like a box of chocolates

At school, we are indoctrinated from a young age to pick one thing.

'What do you want to be when you grow up?' I asked my daughter Amira when she was three.

'A dancer, a postman and part of the PAW Patrol,' she answered

'Wonderful,' I said, because I want to keep cultivating that she can be whatever the heck she likes!

The whole idea that we have to pick certain courses to gear us towards one career that we will be stuck in for the rest of our lives is ludicrous – it's like being told that we can only pick one chocolate from the chocolate box. First, as children, we haven't even had the chance to fully experience the beauty of living life, so how can we possibly know what we want to do? When we try to pick one thing, it's like trying to fit the limitless ocean into a teeny-tiny box. And then children pick careers that sound good or successful – ones their parents encourage them to go for – or panic-choose something because, deep down, they feel they are failing societal norms if they don't know what they want to do.

This is a recipe for disaster and is the perfect storm to make people feel unhappy. If you are not living in accordance with your dharma, you will get feelings of being stuck – like you're taking the action and doing, doing, doing, but not really moving forward. The future won't excite you and that sense of surviving, instead of thriving, will become your operating mode. This can be accompanied by feelings of unworthiness, anxiety, depression or simply feeling 'off', creating dis-ease or a lack of ease in your life.

When our lives feel tough, it begins to take a toll on our physical body, and there is a body of evidence now showing that stress is one of the leading causes of cancer. So if stress is exacerbating physical problems, does it not make perfect sense that we should collectively be looking at how we can reduce it? We should be encouraging our children to tap into and use their unique gifts, instead of pushing them towards a job for the sake of security. This is how we support them in being truly successful and keep them thriving, physically and mentally.

When you are living your dharma, you experience feelings of satisfaction with the way you are expressing and sharing your unique gifts, and you know that you're touching the lives you are meant to touch. On top of that, our unique purpose is the way in which we can create most abundance. It is the easiest way for us to create our own success, manifest the money we desire and give meaning and happiness to our lives.

That acorn never dreams about becoming cherry blossom because its dharma is to become an oak tree. I never dreamed about being an astrophysicist or vet, because these jobs weren't for me. It was in May 2014 that I was by the swimming pool in Bali on my honeymoon. Because I was committed to showing up *on purpose*, I decided to get better at sales in my current job. I had picked up a book on sales from my mother's bookshelf, which was like a treasure chest of personal development, and took it with me to Bali.

The author was a sales trainer and he talked of how he travelled the world coaching people, delivering seminars and changing lives. Every single hair on my body stood up, and this feeling of spiritual electricity rushed through my body. 'I want to do this,' I thought. I didn't really know what that looked like or how I'd make money from it, but that didn't matter – I could *feel* that it was right for me. It made no sense, but life doesn't need to be logical. Our brains can only comprehend a fraction of what is possible for us, but we need to trust those dreams in our minds and the nudges we get. I came to learn that those goosebumps were a signal from my higher self that this was the right journey for me.

It took me two years to get from that idea in May 2014 to heading back to university to study coaching and finally launching my coaching business. I tried my damn hardest to self-sabotage my dream by letting fear get in the way. But by June 2017 I had made my first

£100k while working from home, having coached dozens of people. Since then, my business has grown to help tens of thousands across the globe and has led me to this very moment, when you are reading this page.

Your dharma will help you create abundance of all sorts, but it will also enable you to make the money you desire in order to fuel your dreams. But before we delve into the *how*, it's important that we start off by discussing something of the utmost importance – the reality of reality. Be prepared to have your mind blown.

4.

The truth, the whole truth and
nothing like the truth

My daughter came back from school one day excited to tell me that
she had been learning about solids and liquids during her science
lesson.

'Darling, tell your teacher that nothing is actually solid,' I said
while laughing slightly facetiously.

'Huh?' she said, her innocent little face looking at me, bemused.

I explained to my daughter that quantum physicists discovered
that if you took the strongest microscope and observed an atom,
you would see a small tornado-like vortex, with a number of teeny-
tiny energy vortices called quarks and photons. 'These are what
make up the structure of the atom,' I told her.

I continued to explain that if you focused in closer on the struc-
ture of the atom, you would observe a physical void. The truth is
that the atom has no real solid structure, and atoms are made out of
vibrating invisible energy, therefore they are not actually solid. So if
everything is made of atoms, and atoms aren't actually solid, then
nothing can be actually solid.

'It's quite the conundrum, isn't it, my darling?' I said to my daugh-
ter, who had already switched off when I started talking about
quarks and photons.

From a young age we are taught that, as humans, we are solid
matter, living in a solid world, and we subscribe to the Newtonian
view of science in our education system. I'm sorry to have to be the
one to break your solid bubble, but we have been indoctrinated to
live a life based on a *fundamental lie*. 'A lie?' you say. Yes, a lie.

It has been written about before, over and over again, but it
cannot be emphasized enough: the world of quantum physics sheds

light on the truth about our world in ways that challenge the status quo and everything that your science teacher told you at school. 'But what the hell have atoms, and whether the world is solid or not, to do with creating success?' you may be thinking.

As I began deepening my own spiritual journey and trying to make sense of what I was discovering, I found a few concepts particularly useful as I wrapped my head around 'manifesting'. The first thing I found particularly useful was the fact that even to this very day, all the greatest scientists on this planet – Nobel Prize-winning laureates and physicists – cannot find a universally agreed-upon understanding of the nature of reality. In layman's terms, no one can agree on this pretty important thing.

I will never claim to stack up intellectually with any of the scientists who have put forward their mind-boggling theories, but I found it fascinating to 'play around' with some of the more interesting perspectives, some of which I'll share with you in this chapter, as they helped me grapple with the idea that our thoughts can become things.

For example, take Max Planck, the renowned physicist who was awarded the Nobel Prize for Physics in 1918. As the founder of quantum theory, he expressed an intriguing viewpoint on reality and consciousness. He suggested that consciousness plays a fundamental role in shaping reality. According to Planck, consciousness is not merely an emergent property of matter, but rather a fundamental aspect that gives rise to the physical world.

Then take Albert Einstein, one of the most influential physicists of all time. He proposed that matter and energy curve the fabric of space-time, and that the curvature of space-time in turn influences the motion of matter and energy. For Einstein, the nature of reality was deeply intertwined with the geometry of space-time.

Then there's Roger Penrose, who won the Nobel Prize for Physics in 2020. According to his viewpoint, the nature of reality encompasses both the quantum realm and the subjective experiences of conscious beings. And there's Frank Wilczek, who received the Nobel Prize for Physics in 2004 for his work on the strong nuclear force and who has voiced his interest in the possibility of a multiverse – yep, the whole multiple Spider-Man theory, this dude actually believes that to be true. He rather cleverly and prominently discusses the idea of multiple universes and the implications they might have for our understanding of the cosmos!

And if that hasn't already caused your mind to spontaneously combust, then you won't want to hear that Nick Bostrom, a philosopher and professor at the University of Oxford, has written extensively about the simulation hypothesis. In his influential paper 'Are You Living in a Computer Simulation?', published in 2003, Bostrom presents a philosophical argument suggesting that it is more likely than not that we are living in a computer simulation.

In a nutshell, there are many perspectives and theories from many of the greatest minds. And I believe the story of your life and how it pans out will depend on how you, as an individual, choose to see the nature of reality. If these clever guys can't agree, then I am certainly not going to believe the troll on the internet who pops up to debunk manifesting and the 'law of attraction' as bollocks!

Instead, as I embarked on changing my life, I found it valuable and useful to 'play around' with trying on the theories that resonated most with me and empowered me. I came to see that the truth of life lies only in our perceptions and the perspective that we choose to subscribe to. 'The truth will set you free,' they say, and for me it truly did, when I chose to believe that I had power, and I was wanting to learn how to use it.

Shaping your own reality

For me, personally, the revelation that the universe is not solid as suggested by traditional Newtonian physics, but instead comes from an entanglement of immaterial energy, began to shape a new understanding of who I was and of my place in this universe. The concept that matter and energy are interchangeable, as explained by Einstein's famous equation $E = mc^2$, demonstrates that energy (E) and mass (m) are two forms of the same underlying entity rather than separate. This is where the whole 'the world is actually not solid' theory came from.

Quantum mechanics is the branch of physics that describes the behaviour of matter and energy at the atomic and subatomic level. It provides a theoretical framework that supports the idea of particles possessing both wave-like and particle-like properties, highlighting the interplay between matter and energy. The Danish physicist Niels Bohr said, 'If quantum mechanics hasn't profoundly shocked you, you haven't understood it yet. Everything we call real is made of things that cannot be regarded as real.' This is not new information, but the reality is that *our reality is not what we think it is in reality*. Try saying that fast three times after a couple of beers!

In recent years many scientists have questioned the implications of what has been discovered with quantum physics, and the meaning for us as humans and how we create our own extraordinary lives. One of the potential revelations is that 'the observer creates reality'. This revelation has helped me change my life, and it will help change yours too.

Come again? Yep, I'm about to blow your mind.

One powerful example is the double-slit experiment concerning how waves and particles behave. This experiment illustrated that our consciousness has a role in creating our physical reality (which we now know not to be so physical). This experiment has been used multiple times and has proven that the observation of energy changes the way it behaves. In addition, the famous physicist Sir Arthur Eddington is quoted as saying, 'I believe that the mind has the power to effect groups of atoms and even tamper with the odds of atomic behaviour and that even the course of the world is not predetermined by physical laws, but may be altered by the volition of human beings.'

When we allow ourselves to fully comprehend this idea, it becomes simply breathtaking. The significance of this information is for us to wake up and realize that we are all energy, radiating our own unique energy-signature, and we are creating our lives every second of the day.

Studies have proven that different states of emotion (driven by our thoughts) result in different electromagnetic frequencies, which then have an impact on changing the state of other atoms. In a nutshell, as observers, we are personally involved in the creation of our own reality, which supports the ideas of some of the clever-ass scientists I referenced earlier in this chapter (see page 30).

The more I read and researched, the more I began to see that this whole manifestation-of-your-life thing isn't as woo-woo or as esoteric as you might think, and that there's some real data that lends itself to the theory that our thoughts literally can become things.

We are not a product of our lives, but our lives are in fact a product of us. *Read that again.*

Put us under a microscope and you will see that each human is made up of approximately seven octillion vibrating atoms. As the very smart inventor and engineer Nikola Tesla said, 'If you want to know the secrets of the universe, think in terms of energy, frequency and vibration.' But since everything in our universe is made of these vibrating atoms of energy, what makes us different from, say, a book or a mug?

Well, there is a life force that makes us animate, living, breathing humans and not just skin and bones. It's like we are all unique domain names being hosted on a main server, making us 'live' on the human internet. Every human is hosted by this main server, but each unique domain represents a different human experience. This host gives us consciousness, which means that, unlike a book, we are able to feel and breathe and have thoughts. We are all hosted by that same energy force, until our time on this planet expires and that consciousness decides to move on, and our bodies are . . . well, dead.

So what is this host that I speak of? The reality is that, no matter how hard we try to find a definitive answer, I like to see it as the consciousness that is referred to by scientists such as Max Planck. I also think it's safe to say that unless I can track down the creator of everything, and coerce them to spill the beans on how the heck we all ended up here, we need to agree on one thing: we ain't gonna know. It's a deeply philosophical question, debated over millennia, and since the smartest minds on this planet cannot agree on it, I certainly don't have a chance.

But here's how I like to see it. I'm not a religious person, but as I see the beautiful sun come up each day without ever taking a day off, and the four seasons changing flawlessly year in, year out, and as I witness my incredible body creating and birthing life multiple times, I've come to the conclusion that there is an intelligence working backstage to orchestrate the sheer magic of everything on this planet. Whatever is hosting me has intelligence beyond comprehension. But just because I believe that, *you* don't need to. One thing I've come to realize is that you do not need to believe it for its magic to work.

We can call this intelligence 'source energy', the life force, spirit or consciousness. And some may want to call it God. The word doesn't matter; it's a recognition that we are connected to something bigger than ourselves. It's through that consciousness we are all being hosted by that we have the powerful ability to shape our reality.

*Flipping the f*cking switch*

Have you ever heard yourself saying things like 'When I have X, then I'll do X, and then I'll finally be happy'? Most humans live life with the internal story that being happy is the end-goal only after the attainment of X, Y and Z.

Imagine someone standing on the shore, gazing out at the vast ocean. In the distance, they spot a beautiful horizon. The person believes that once they reach that horizon, they will finally experience success. They set off on a journey, putting in tremendous effort and facing various challenges along the way. As they approach the horizon, it seems to move further away, no matter how much progress they make. The person keeps pushing forward, convinced their happiness lies just beyond the horizon. But no matter how far they travel, the horizon remains elusive.

Like attaining the horizon, people believe that the achievement of goals will be the answer to long-lasting happiness and fulfilment. We are taught that when we *have* what we want, then we can *do* what we want and we will finally *be* this super-successful human, ticking all the boxes of society's expectations because people attach their happiness to external conditions or future achievements, believing they need to attain certain things to be happy, But I can tell you now that there's more of a chance of seeing a unicorn taking a piss in your bathroom than of you creating abundance in your life if you operate from this system.

As I dived into the fascinating world of quantum physics and learned that this *have, do, be* model of creating my life was never going to work, then flipped the f*cking switch on its head, my life changed drastically.

You see, we are called human *beings*, and so starting off with *being* is the first crucial step to creating success. When we can *be*, we can start to have an effect on the atoms around us and thus start this process of creating our own reality. I learned that the frequency of our vibration determines what we attract, as expounded by the law of attraction, which states that 'like attracts like'. The way we 'be' will directly affect our experience of life and what we will ultimately achieve.

For my part, I needed to 'be' successful (internally send out that vibration), then 'do' the things I needed to do (take action) externally, and then I'd 'have' all the things I'd dreamed of, because my consciousness has a direct impact on my physical reality.

It makes sense that we are called human beings, not human doings, and we need to learn to 'be' before we can 'do' and 'have'. This is how we manifest our desires into reality. The more you can cultivate a feeling of success from the inside out, the more material measures of success you will create in the external world; but most of us are wanting to create success from a place of lack, scarcity and fear, operating as a humanoid in survival mode. What we never get taught as children is that our physical world is like a projection of our inner world. It's like a printout of a document that you typed up in your earlier years.

Let me give you an example. Let's say my editor wanted to read this chapter, so I printed it off, as I wanted to send him a physical copy. The reality is that once I'd printed it off, I'd notice some typos, which is standard Noor behaviour. So I'd then ask my kids if I could borrow their eraser so that I could rub out the typos. So here I am, trying to rub out typos on the hard copy I've printed off for my editor, and then I press print again.

What would happen? Well, duh, Noor! Obviously the same document with the same typos would come out. I could take a bigger eraser, or study the best way to erase, and no matter what I did on that hard copy of the manuscript it would never change how it would look when printed out. The only way I could change those typos was by going back into Google Docs (the program) and changing it at the source.

Our external successes – money, health and love – are all results. We live in a world of cause and effect, so we need to start understanding the cause, which begins from within.

The process of *being* starts with being consciously aware. This gives you the power to observe when your decisions in life are driven by true desire or by your ego's need to fit in and be better than others, which is a sign that you are operating from the wrong mode, my friend. There is nothing wrong with wanting nice things; if they bring you joy and are aligned with your vision for your most successful life, then nice things can make you feel good, and that feeling will help you to emit a higher vibration and keep you aligned with the future you want to create.

So if you want to buy fancy items, that's completely fine as long as you are doing it with conscious awareness, and out of desire, not out of fear that somehow you aren't good enough *without those things*. That's why, in this book, I'd love to give you the most incredibly powerful transformational life tools, which helped me become a 'success'.

I want to guide you inwards and help you define success on your terms. I'll provide you with a lost instruction manual to take back your power, so that you can consciously create a life better than in your wildest dreams.

But before we do that, I'd like to help you understand *why* you are the person you have become today. This is the first part of becoming aware and breaking free from the shackles of our humanoid behaviour. Instead of following the lead of your parents and grandparents, all of whom were guided by society as to what is normal, you need to let go of these norms, which don't actually set you up to succeed. With this new awareness, you will see why your life is the way it is, and how to change to get where you want to be in the future. As I said previously, we are vibratory humans, emitting energy and shaping our lives.

So what governs how fast we vibrate, and to which frequency?

Our thoughts.

And what precedes our thoughts?

Our beliefs.

And how are our beliefs created?

Well, for the most part our beliefs are created in our childhood.

We give meaning and create mental scripts that reside in our subconscious mind in relation to situations that we see, hear and experience as children. These scripts create the stories and beliefs that become the lens through which we see life and the way we operate, because our thoughts drive our actions, and our actions create our results.

Our beliefs are how we give meaning to our world and experience. They are the stories we tell ourselves about who we are and what we can achieve – our 'subconscious scripts'. They guide how we see ourselves and create a mental image. If life was a movie and you were the main actor, your scripts would guide the way you should perform and therefore the movie of your life.

So before we delve into defining success or creating a life that is aligned with that, let's take a little journey backwards and look at how you became the person you are today, and why you haven't perhaps created the success you desire. Let's explore your own stories and scripts, which have formed the filter through which you see the world.

It's time to wake up and become aware of your subconscious scripts and how they have held you back. This awareness alone will change the trajectory of your life!

5.

Subconscious scripts

I dreamed about passing my driving test and getting my first car from the minute I turned seventeen. I was desperate for a car, so when my parents generously presented me with a second-hand little Fiat Punto, I felt like I'd arrived at adulthood. Even though it was nothing fancy, it was mine. I went straight to Halfords and used my savings to buy some new hubcaps to make it look like the car had alloy wheels, so that I felt like my friends at school with their spangly new cars.

I remember how much I used to love cleaning the Fiat, with a sense of pride. I'd pour the water on and then glide a yellow sponge across the body, and as it soaked up all the dirt, I'd watch with deep satisfaction as the dirty water drained out of the sponge with every gentle squeeze. When I think back on that, it reminds me of what we are like as children. Between the ages of two and eight we are like a sponge, soaking up all of life's adventures; everything we see, hear and experience penetrates our minds, seeping into us and moulding us into the people we are today. This becomes the filter through which we will operate in our lives. Let's call this filter your 'paradigm'.

Your paradigm is made up of beliefs, values and attitudes about *everything*: your stories. It's an internal GPS guiding your thoughts, actions and behaviour on autopilot. It's like a huge book tucked in the corners of your mind, filled with stories about relationships, success, money, love, food, sex and the body. This list is by no means exhaustive. If you were an actor in a film, your paradigm would hold the scripts you read that create the movie of your life. It's the filter through which you see the world and consequently make decisions about everything that you experience as a human being. Like the software program in your computer, what is inputted will be responsible for what shows up on the screen of your life. Your paradigm will either pull you towards or push you away from your goals, because it's the unconscious yet powerful driving force behind your whole life.

Just as each pore of a sponge gets heavier as the water and dirt mix together and penetrate it, so we, as humans, become heavier over time, carrying about the baggage of our past. Consequently when life begins to push pressure on us, everything that seeped into us during our younger years – the good, the bad and f*cking ugly – will begin to pour out, just as it does from a sponge, and create our reality. Unfortunately, for most of us, what pours out is dirty water, filled with fear, scarcity, limitations and confusion. We don't consciously want muddy water to leak into our lives, washing away our potential and our dreams, but we don't even realize this is happening. That's why your current life is a direct reflection of your paradigm, aka your *unconscious* identity.

Why does this happen?

In case you are new to my books or my work, or maybe even to personal development, I want to offer a quick synopsis of the basics concerning how and why we are the way we are. This will bode well as you embark on your journey of transforming every area of your life. And even if you are not new to this, hearing about it over and over again will serve you well when it comes to remembering how powerful you truly are and yet how powerless you can be, if left to your own programmed devices.

We all have a brain, although after four kids and a decade of broken sleep, mine sometimes feels like it's filled with mashed potatoes, with Cocomelon songs on repeat, living rent-free in my head! Your brain is that powerful pulsating organ that is yet to be fully understood by even the greatest scientists on this planet. It is the control centre where stimulus is interpreted, and the processing centre for the raw data of the world. The brain is a database and data processor, storing the plethora of experiences we've had from the time we were born.

Since no one can agree on how the mind differs from the brain, the way I like to look at it is that the brain is the physical part of the mind, and there's a non-physical part of the mind too. They are inextricably linked. The mind is not physical or tangible, it cannot be dissected in a science lab, but it's the powerful operating force behind our lives. There are two levels of the mind: our conscious mind and our subconscious mind.

Our conscious and subconscious minds

Our *conscious mind* is the logical and creative part, but contrary to popular belief, it accounts for a mere 5 per cent of how we operate. Our conscious mind is where our personality dwells: the 'I' that walks around every day, talking to other people. When you think of who 'you' are, this is the part of yourself that you usually identify with. However, that 'you' is only the part of your identity that is visible and conscious to you. Beneath that conscious mind – that identity and the thoughts and feelings that we consciously associate with – there is another layer containing deeper aspects of yourself; these are the subconscious scripts that have carved our personality. The conscious mind is only the tip of the iceberg floating above the sea. It is the subconscious mind that is the vast mountain of ice lurking beneath the surface.

It is in our *subconscious mind* that our paradigm lives: the internal concept of self, others and the world, and the engine that automates our behaviour. It is responsible for the remaining 95 per cent of the outcomes in our physical world. It is our personality outside our awareness, secretly controlling much of what we say, believe and do. It is the personality that creates our own reality, and the fuel that runs that engine of the subconscious mind consists of our *beliefs*.

Up until the age of eight, our conscious mind has not formed and our subconscious mind is like that sponge: its pores are open and ready to receive and integrate all incoming experiences. Everything we see, hear and experience we absorb and we become programmed by our parents, religion, society, the medical industry, the government and our education. Each experience in our childhood causes nerve cells called neurons to fire up, creating networks in our brains. Unlike the conscious mind, the subconscious mind accepts everything that is impressed upon it, and you can plant the seeds of a beautiful rose bush or the seeds of a poisonous weed in the soil of the subconscious. It will accept either one with no questions and will either nurture a great belief or one that can be poisonous.

As children, we give meaning to our individual experiences with everything, from food to our parents' relationship, to money, sex and our bodies. These meanings create simplified stories in our minds, planting seeds in the soil of our subconscious, resulting in it sprouting beliefs even without us knowing. When our parents tell us, 'Don't waste food' or 'Money doesn't grow on trees', or we witness our parents arguing, or we get bullied at school for being different, we decide what each of these things mean, in a simplified version.

Our subconscious mind learns through repetition and so, as we experience the same things in our lives, such as parents constantly arguing about money, those neurons organize themselves into patterns with long-lasting connections. If we encounter a repeated thought, behaviour or feeling, it will soon turn into an unconscious habit, and we have then become hardwired to be the person we are.

These subconscious beliefs form our attitudes and evolve to become habits. Our habits then guide our actions, and ultimately our actions result in our outcomes. Raise your hand if you came from a generation when you were told to finish your plate of food? Even if you felt stuffed, you were told not to waste food and to finish it up, so you did, because the grown-ups said so. That belief that we must finish our plate of food, even when we feel full, has created adults who aren't able to portion-control or finish eating when they feel satisfied, which has resulted in over-eating. This powerful subconscious script runs in the background and, like an invisible force, inhibits people from losing weight, no matter how much they diet. Thus our subconscious mind and the stories that we have will be a huge factor in whether or not we create success in every area of life, because even if we have conscious desires, if our subconscious mind is not on board and has a conflicting story, then the subconscious mind will win.

In addition, it rules your emotions because your experiences are filtered through it. Therefore your paradigm can make you feel happy or it can make you feel sad. It can increase your energy and motivate you to great heights, or it can suppress your energy and keep you feeling depressed and miserable. Because emotions directly affect your physical functioning, your subconscious mind can make you sick or it can keep you well. Yes, it is that freaking powerful.

The subconscious mind has four primary functions, and understanding them is so important for creating a life on your own terms:

1. Safety and survival
2. Conserving energy
3. Moving away from pain
4. Moving towards pleasure.

As we go through life, our mind/brain collects and categorizes the millions of bytes of incoming information that it decodes from our five senses. Light waves, sound waves and the electromagnetic resistance that we experience when we touch other vibratory objects in the world all get decoded by the brain. It then turns that raw data into a form we understand: thoughts.

Most of us spend each day in very similar environments, experiencing for the most part the same people as we did in the days, months and years before. Therefore, environmentally, not much changes. An average person thinks 60,000–70,000 thoughts a day, but 90 per cent of those thoughts are the same, because they are simply a response to the environment that your brain is decoding at every given second, and therefore our responses (thoughts) tend to be similar on a day-to-day basis. We may believe we are consciously thinking our thoughts and choosing what we think, but in actual fact our thoughts are simply a response to external stimuli perceived by our senses – a reaction rather than a creation.

With every piece of information that comes flowing into us, our minds seek to match it up to something relevant from our past, so the mind becomes like our very own Google search engine. This all happens super-super-fast, and below the level of conscious awareness. When we encounter something unknown that our brains don't easily find a match for, in the space of milliseconds we will have a thought that is followed by a response in our physical body – known to us as an emotion.

I once heard someone refer to an emotion as 'energy in motion' and, since we are all energetic beings, that made complete sense to me. When we experience an emotion, we give meaning to the experience of that energy moving in our bodies – and the meanings that we give it we refer to as our feelings.

Decoding your emotions

Emotions are sensations, the raw physical data and a reaction to the present reality, which serve the purpose of getting us to do something. We believe these sensations to be 100 per cent accurate pieces of information that we should bow down to and abide by – which, as you will soon see, is not what is happening.

Once we experience the sensations, we then say things like 'I feel scared', giving meaning to what is now happening in the body. However, feelings are filtered through our paradigm and the stories we've created, based on events from the past – and not necessarily on the truth of the situation. That's because our subconscious mind (where our paradigm lives) does not know the difference between past, present and future. This is one of the most important facets of the subconscious mind that we need to understand if we are to create success. What I would love to share is a perspective about how the mind works that has revolutionized my life, and those of my clients. Recognizing that the mind is prone to dysfunction, and that this dysfunction happens in most people, enabled me to understand why logically we may think something, yet our body reacts in a conflicting manner and we feel scared, tense or resistant.

For example, you may decide to start a new business venture because you are fed up with the nine-till-five rat race. First and foremost, since the mind's primary function is safety and survival, starting something new means that you are attempting to stride outside your comfort zone and into the wild Wild West of the unknown.

Your conscious mind thinks, 'I'm so excited to start a new business venture.'

The subconscious mind searches through the past-history files of your personal mind autobiography to find when you last started a new business venture. It may struggle to find an exact match that setting up a new business venture will be successful and that leaving your nice safe job is a good idea, because the likelihood is that you have never done this before.

So the mind finds an old story that's almost been etched into the dark corners of the mind. You were four, and you tried something new at school and it didn't work out and you felt horrible sensations, such as shame. Since the subconscious mind likes to categorize anything that is even slightly structurally similar, within an instant the sirens in your mind go off.

The subconscious mind alerts the nervous system, 'Potential virus – please shut down immediately.' It signals Risk with a capital R: risk of failure, risk of disappointment, risk of making ourselves look like complete idiots. The mind can be dramatic and over-protective, like a bouncer outside a nightclub, and will stop you from entering unknown territories where you could risk being unsafe.

If we are faced with something that could potentially cause us pain or rock our security blanket of life, the sympathetic nervous system will be activated and, in the space of milliseconds, we will start to feel the symptoms of our fight-or-flight response kicking in, as chemicals begin flooding our bodies to warn us that things could go wrong if we continue to move in this direction. These chemicals create uncomfortable emotions, such as fear and anxiety, and we begin to make them mean something. And because there is no actual threat to flee from, we end up freezing. This is why so many humans feel stuck.

Could it be that we're caught in a gunfight in the Wild West of the unknown land of business ventures? The subconscious mind reacts as though we are, and since the last thing we want is to get caught up in the crossfire, it prevents us moving forward.

Because our minds filter all our desires through our subconscious stories that we created as children, they will seek to find *any* experiences when we perhaps failed in the past and will remind us that we don't want to feel that shame or embarrassment again. And it's easy for the mind to find these experiences, because the subconscious mind does not function to perfection. There is a glitch in the way it processes stuff. As adults, many of us can think of a negative experience as a child and we can relive and feel the emotion as though it is happening today. That is because the subconscious mind hasn't actually processed that information properly. It's like a tab being left open on your computer screen of your mind, draining energy. And since it doesn't know the difference between past, present and future, the subconscious mind believes that what happened then is still happening now. This is why we feel all the negative emotions flooding us, and the nervous system overworking to keep us safe.

'You cannot leave your nice safe, secure job to set up a business that you don't know will be a success,' we hear ourselves say, after our bodies feel the stress hormone cortisol running through them, in response to the desire to set up a new business.

Because our bodies have responded to the mere thought (which is a perceived threat) of setting up a business as if it's a real threat, like facing tigers and lions and bears in the depth of the jungle, we may say things like, 'I feel scared it won't be successful.' Announcing these feelings creates a negative feedback loop to the brain, which confirms those initial *false* thoughts that setting up a business is scary and to be avoided. 'Get back in your bloody comfort zone!' our bodies scream at us.

And so we do. We do not like the sensation of discomfort in our bodies or the mysteries of unknown pastures. So we retreat to safety, back to our cosy sofas and Netflix programmes. And that is how we get stuck in a vicious cycle of mediocrity in life, forever remaining a creature of habit operating in survival mode.

This is why so many of us procrastinate about taking action. As you can see, emotions and feelings are often used interchangeably, but there is a difference. Emotions come first, then feelings follow, as the emotion chemicals go to work in our bodies. We then get flooded with thoughts about everything that could go wrong, as our brains cleverly catastrophize the idea of leaving the security of a nine-to-five job to start up a business.

Stepping outside your comfort zone

As you go through this book, you will see that creating success is usually right outside our comfort zone – and the brain perceives anything outside our comfort zone as unsafe, and therefore as a big fat f*cking no-go area. It's like we are hardwired for hardship, instead of built to succeed. 'How does this happen?' you may ask. If we are built for success, then why do our brains and bodies shut down when we try to escape Groundhog Day, break the mould and step out of our oh-so-comfortable zone?

First, as children we learned that in order to meet our basic needs for love, we shouldn't disappoint our parents, teachers or society. Why? Because we are hardwired to feel safe, and making sure that our caregivers aren't disappointed is part of staying safe. When we are faced with something that could potentially end up in us feeling disappointed with ourselves or disappointing others, our minds remind us of all the times when we did something wrong as children, or failed at something, and adults told us they were disappointed in us. Sometimes they did not even need to say that word – it was merely a look or a feeling that we got from them.

'Why did you fail that exam? You should have tried harder.'
'You should have scored that goal – that was an easy one.'
'Stop crying, you're causing a scene.'
My daughter Layla-Rose is one of those children who can't bear

the thought of disappointing someone. She is very well behaved, and the teachers all say what a delight she is. However, I noticed that she has a really deep fear of getting told off, mainly by people outside her family. During one of our school-run conversations I began probing, and I found out something pivotal concerning why she felt this fear.

She recalled that in nursery, when she was just three years old, she was using playdough and had made some pretend food. In her childhood silliness, she put the playdough in her mouth, taking her role-playing a bit further than one would desire. Instead of politely and calmly dealing with her, her nursery teacher got angry and shouted at her. Layla-Rose recalled this in vivid detail, even though it was years later. 'I didn't mean to eat it. I just forgot it was play-dough, and the teacher got so mad and told the whole class not to eat playdough like I had done.'

The teacher had told her off because of course she could have choked, but because she got very angry and publicly announced to her classmates what Layla-Rose had done, my little girl was left processing a mixture of emotions as a three-year-old – disappointment and shame. The compound of these two emotions locked into her subconscious mind. That feeling was so difficult for her to process as a small child, and her brain locked it in and told her to avoid anything in future that could bring up those feelings again.

My daughter's extremely good behaviour had become a defence mechanism. While I don't want my child to misbehave, I don't want her to shy away from breaking rules from time to time, either! When it comes to creating outrageous success, we need to be a bit of a rule- and system-breaker and do things that others might deem out of the ordinary, and that could involve disappointing someone.

That episode in nursery might seem trivial to us, but it was a pivotal moment of trauma for Layla-Rose, and the first time she had experienced a compound of negative emotions leading her to feel unsafe. Our brain sucks up and stores those moments and tucks them neatly in our subconscious mind, creating the filter through which we will decide whether or not to go forth. It wants us to avoid all situations later on that could bring up that emotion again.

So when we think about pursuing a new venture that might not end up the way we wish, the discomfort of disappointment is something that our brains want to move us away from, so we stop and create the convincing story in our heads that we need to retreat to our comfort zone, wearing our PJs and fluffy slippers. We park the dream of escaping the rat race till next year, telling ourselves that somehow we will be more ready then.

Sound familiar?

Changing our lives means changing what we believe, so that we can change how we behave; but changing what we believe is not something that can be done at the click of a finger. We have become conditioned to who we are over the years – we have become creatures of habit, hardwired to create the reality that we are currently living. The reason we work on autopilot is that one of the primary functions of the brain is to conserve energy, and working on autopilot means that we don't need to 'waste' energy consciously doing the tasks we do on a daily basis, such as brushing our teeth and making cups of tea.

Creating new beliefs requires consciously breaking the automatic negative feedback loops that have made us the person we are today. Consciously trying to change requires willpower. However, willpower is a limited resource of energy (think of when you have tried to force yourself to get to the gym!) and when we run out of it, we bounce back to who we were. This is why most people fail at achieving their goals and transforming their lives. We go back to responding and reacting to life and our environments, rather than *creating a new life*.

The subconscious mind works to turn your strongest expectations into reality, so if you have a belief that creating success or money is bad (and yes, we will look at why most people see success as a bad thing later on), you will see life through this lens and will seek experiences to confirm your beliefs. This is called 'confirmation bias' in psychology.

Because your subconscious mind is responsible for your emotions, and your emotions affect your vibration, it is heavily involved in whether you manifest what you desire in life. When we experience emotions, we either vibrate at a higher or a lower frequency. Ever been around someone and thought, 'Sheesh, they are so low-vibe' or 'Wow, they are so high-vibe'? That's because we are all literally emitting energy, and we can feel it!

The law of attraction states that 'like attracts like'. And yes, I do believe in the law of attraction, but it is one of many laws of the universe that I will cover in greater depth later on. And even if you've stuck up your nose at this concept as being woo-woo, I'm confident I'll get you to have a different perspective when you have read my case.

As I've deepened my understanding around manifestation and the way the mind works, I want to bring to you another level of the mind – we will call this level the *super-conscious mind*: the mind of our spiritual self, our soul.

Our spiritual mind is the part connected to the greater infinite intelligence and life force, and when we close our eyes and enter the quantum field, we can connect with that. Our spiritual mind is where we can use our imagination to create our reality, and where our intuition and our ideas initiate. It is the part of the mind that we didn't get given an instruction manual for, and yet it is the part that – when accessed, trusted and used in the right way – can help us create a life better than our goddamn dreams, and all the money we desire.

The thing is, money truly makes the world go round, but it is misunderstood by us all. We believe that money is a mark of how successful we are, and to some degree there is merit in that, because if we are living our purpose and making money, that money represents how many people we have helped. But why do we struggle to create money? Well, we have talked already about how the paradigm affects our lives, and I will go deeper into this subject in Part Three of the book, because once you grasp this, it has the power to change *everything*.

In Part Two we are going to explore the method for manifesting the abundance we desire, and for creating what I like to call a 'Fuck, yes!' life.

PART TWO

The Method

6.

The 'Fuck, yes!' life

We all deserve a 'Fuck, yes!' life – the kind of life where we pinch ourselves because we aren't quite sure if it's real. But here's the deal . . . You want to know the biggest secret of creating that kind of life, with epic success, full of 'Fuck, yes!' moments? It's less about getting to a destination, and requires that you truly enjoy the journey. Yep, that's more of a cliché and more cheesy than a goddamn selection of Camemberts on Christmas Day, but it's the truth.

In this second part of the book we are going to examine *how* to create a 'Fuck, yes!' life, and I'll be sharing the exact method that I've used to transform my desires into reality, time and again. This is a process that I've taught to thousands of people, and those who have committed to implementing it have seen radical changes in their lives.

By learning the art of curating your *Vision*, the importance of aligning your *Identity* and the power of taking *Action*, life can seem to change magically in front of your very eyes. But it's not magic; it's a process that's worked time and time again for thousands of people in my world. That's why I took the process and created the 'VIA Manifesting Method®', whose three core pillars are Vision, Identity and Action. We will look at how to change your life the VIA way, and why it will help you to transform your thoughts into physical reality.

The video game of life

One of my favourite analogies is to imagine that life is like a video game. There are infinite levels that you can transcend and at each level there will be a new prize to collect, a new baddy to fight and a new obstacle to challenge you. There will be a new skill that you can acquire, and it gets harder to avoid the things that could kill you; but the more you play, the stronger you become and the higher the levels that you transcend!

Once you know the rules of the game and expect the unexpected, life can become a fun challenge of growth and accomplishment. While attaining the flag at the end is a glorious achievement, it's playing the game that is the best part. I used to think that getting to a point where all my goals were complete, and where everything was stable, was the end-goal. But I came to realize that 'stability' is what causes mental chaos, because we don't have anything to strive for. Although success has historically been linked to achievement (which is the experience of accomplishing the things you want in life), that only comes from mastering the skills necessary to produce results (aka the journey).

And let's be honest, most gamers who complete a game do not fling the console across the room and declare it's the last one they will ever play, thereby retiring from their hobby. In fact it's on to the next game, and the next, and the next. Why? Because it's the person you need to become on the road to finding success that is the most interesting and fulfilling. You can play a game for weeks or months, but once you get to the end, that is simply one moment in time. That feeling of achievement is fleeting. When that moment passes, you want to be on that fun journey again. But what makes the journey fulfilling?

Fulfilment is the power to understand, appreciate and enjoy your life, and this comes from creating a life of meaning. Someone may have all the achievements and money in the world but be internally and spiritually bankrupt, because they have been so busy getting to the highest levels of the game that they forgot to enjoy the experience of getting there.

It's like collecting all the stars on that level, but never stopping to appreciate how sparkly they are or the sheer number of points that you accrued with each one you bagged. When we are on the road to success, but forget to look out of the window to appreciate what it took to get there, we miss out on the sweetness of the achievement. Lack of meaning also comes when our primary goal is achievement, but perhaps the route we took to get there didn't fulfil our soul's deeper yearning.

Let me use an Olympic swimmer as an example. Imagine they have trained since childhood to be the fastest and strongest swimmer, have multiple gold medals to represent their achievement, plus sponsorship deals that have financially secured their future for life. But they are not happy. Is something missing? In fact studies have shown that when Olympians go to the Games and they are over, 80 per cent of them have depressive symptoms. Why does this happen? First, because they've lost something to strive for. And perhaps it's because their lives lack a deeper meaning and they yearn for more than simply beating a personal best in a big tank of water. They get the 'Fuck, yes!' from that moment of winning, but perhaps the swimmer hasn't had time to find a relationship or have children, and that's what their heart really yearns for. So the achievement of Olympic medals feels bittersweet. Conversely, you might have a loving spouse and wonderful children and still feel a sense of emptiness, because you haven't honoured your unique blueprint and your purpose in life vocationally.

A holistic approach to success is something that I feel strongly about – we can't simply measure success by someone's net-worth or external achievements, and we cannot seek this end-goal believing it will bring us some sort of stability and peace. We need to be okay with the fact that hustling towards something and having a level of chaos in our lives actually makes us feel alive, because we are growing.

Finding fulfilment

We need to feel fulfilled in all the areas of our lives that matter to us, and we need to honour all parts of our lives in order to enjoy true success. How can we enjoy abundant wealth if we are chronically sick? How can we have a deep and meaningful relationship if we are stressed about finances? How can we celebrate having the best health if we don't have the right people around us to share our lives with and so feel a deep loneliness? We need to focus on all areas of our lives so that we can feel fulfilled across the board.

That's why it's imperative that our success is not measured simply by achievement, and why it has to be *inextricably linked* to fulfilment. Fulfilment comes from a life of meaning – a life where you feel your life matters in some significant way – and studies have shown that this often comes with contributions beyond ourselves to other people. As humans we have needs; our basic needs, driven by our ego, are for survival, but beyond that, we have spiritual needs. These needs drive us to grow in all areas of our lives and to contribute beyond ourselves. Life only matters, and can continue to matter, if we feel that we are fully alive, which is what growth gives us. This is why many people feel unhappy when their lives are like Ground-hog Day, simply going through the motions.

That's why I believe the conversation about success needs to radically change, for our generation and future generations. Let's stop measuring whether someone is successful by the money they earn, the clothes they wear or what the media tries to tell us. I've met some pretty shitty 'successful' people, and no amount of money will make them act like decent human beings. We need to be teaching our children that a life with meaning and purpose is more valuable than likes on the 'gram. That doesn't mean we should down-value the importance of creating wealth, which leads to freedom, because we are all designed to create the abundance we desire (more on this later). But *how* we get there is of paramount importance to our happiness and fulfilment.

Once I started to live my life in alignment with my unique blueprint, I was able to help change the lives of thousands of people across the globe, through living my purpose. The magic secret to creating success comes from pivoting your perspective from 'How do I benefit if I create success?' to 'How can we all benefit if I create success?' When your motivation is rooted in success *beyond* your own personal needs, then you can create the wildest levels of abundance.

My desire to create a coaching business initially stemmed from a deep-rooted desire to help others. Of course there was also a desire to create income for myself and my family. The best part was that by helping others change their minds and their lives, this had a ripple effect on the greater collective, because the impact of the shift in my clients' mindsets impacted on those they love.

The more people I help, the more I earn of course, but it's a win-win for everyone. Those people will go off to create happier, fulfilled lives, and many of them desire to share their wisdom and help others – the ripple effect is pretty awesome! But beyond the financial rewards, an amazing review of one of my books or a private message from a happy client is fuel for my soul, which keeps me turned on and feeling alive. To this day, I still reply personally to all my messages on social media, and it shocks me when people are dumbfounded that it's me answering, as though I'm too important to acknowledge a gorgeous message of gratitude. I live for those moments, so if you ever feel a change in your life as a result of anything I've said and done, then tell me, because I truly love it.

So the next thing I'd love to do is share some of the rules for success that I've come to realize form the foundation for manifesting a 'Fuck, yes!' life.

The VIA Manifesting Method®

First, we need to get really clear about what we desire – not just in one area of our lives, but in eight different areas (see page 69). Once we have created a vision for life that makes us want to jump out of bed and create it, we then need to do the inner work to make sure our subconscious scripts are on board and in alignment, and driving us towards our vision instead of unconsciously repelling it. Lastly, we must take action. We can't just sit and watch the video game and hope we reach the top levels through positive visualization. So we start with *Vision*, we move on to *Identity* and we finish with good old *Action* – the three core pillars that I truly believe we need to dial up and get right, if we want to see massive changes in our lives.

As I've already explained, your vision for your life is not something that you need to come up with from scratch – all the data for what you truly desire lies within you and it's simply about connecting to it. Also, there is a difference between vision and goal-setting, which we will explore in Chapter Eight. Before we do so, I'll leave you with a question that I'd like you to ponder – a question that I often ask my students: 'If you had only faith and no fear, what would you love your life to look like?'

Grab a piece of paper and a pen and spend some time thinking how different your life would look if you weren't scared to go ahead and create it. If you weren't fearful of failure, you weren't worried about the 'how' and you weren't scared that people would judge you. What would that be like?

Immerse yourself in this question, and I'll see you in the next chapter!

7.

Which game are you going to play?

I arrived at my daughter's hockey game and scanned the pitches to see which playing field she was on. I caught a glimpse of her and watched her proudly as she zipped around the pitch, scoring goals with a beaming smile on her face. When she came off the playing field, she informed me proudly that she'd been asked to play with the older girls on a different pitch, as she was one of the strongest hockey players in her class.

Her team won, while her peers who were on a different playing field were defeated by the other school. There was a clear difference in energy and attitude between the teams. The winning-team players believed they could win, played to win and the results reflected that. It really got me thinking about how there seem to be different approaches to living life from an energetic standpoint. Let's imagine there are two different energetic fields to play on in life. Each field represents a different energy or frequency and our choice of how to play will be reflected in the results that we get.

The majority of people in life (the masses) are playing a very safe and predictable game on field number one; let's call this the *field of predictability*. There's nothing wrong with this at all (we need safety and predictability in order to meet our survival needs in life), but the results will always be limited.

On this energetic field, everything has pretty predictable results and most people have their lives planned out, based on what they know and have been taught about progressing in life. They subscribe to a linear way of thinking, bound by logical reasoning and realism around achieving success and higher finances. This usually means they believe there are certain rules to acquiring more success, governed by societal norms – such as more education equals higher pay, and more hours equal more money. There are clear steps for success when you subscribe to the way of life on this field: you get good grades at school, which then predict that you will go to university. You go to university, which then predicts that you may be in with a better chance of getting a good job. You get a job that will most likely be from nine till five, five days a week, with a predictable thirty days' holiday a year. And with this job, which pays X amount of money, you will get an X percentage rise in salary every year, predictably. On this field, time is exchanged for money, and most high-paying jobs usually equate to sixty- or seventy-hour working weeks and lots of stress. Finally, in your sixties you will retire and live off the pension you've saved for your whole life, hopefully to enjoy a few years of 'freedom'.

If you told someone who lives on this energy field that a home-less person could somehow build a multimillion-pound empire, they would laugh, because that's simply not possible and does not fit with their beliefs about success. Especially if that person didn't get good grades. After all, we are told that good grades are the gateway to paradise! This often means that if you don't have a great education, you are most likely limited in what you can earn. Deviating from the rules for creating success as adopted by the masses is simply not an option. On this playing field there are clear and predictable steps to attaining success, and if you don't follow them, then you don't get where you wish to be – unless you decide to become a drug dealer, because that's the only other way to achieve wild wealth on this field and it explains why many people turn to crime to create more money.

Predictability is a comfort blanket for people on this field, even if it means that their dreams stay in their minds for the duration of their lives. This energy feels safe and secure because, at some level, you can control the outcome. There are many people who will go through life doing this and won't bat an eyelid. I spent numerous years like most people on this field, going about my life like I was 'meant' to. But for me it felt restrictive, and I couldn't help but wonder, 'Is this it?' My soul yearned for more.

I did all the things that were meant to get me to 'success', but something never felt right. First, after university I had zero clue about what the hell I wanted to do, so as we've seen, I decided to flee to the Mediterranean and work as a Club 18–30 rep. I did this for six years, before falling pregnant and having to resume my former predictable life, which everyone else seemed to live in, by taking a job I hated so that we could survive. But I wanted more; and when you want more, you begin to unlock the entry point to the next field – a very different energy when it comes to playing the game of life.

As I started to explore other options on the internet for potential careers or business ideas, as I hatched my escape plan from the job that I loathed, it was like I went to my wardrobe to pick out an outfit for my f*cking predictable life and I noticed that at the back of my wardrobe was a door I'd never seen before. I opened the door and – *Holy macaroni!* – entered some sort of Narnia and suddenly saw things that I could never un-see, and people living a life that was very different from the one I was accustomed to.

I saw people earning £10,000 a month, living in their pyjamas and selling their own brand of products online from the comfort of their own homes. I saw mums travelling six times a year with their brood of children while selling e-books from a laptop. I observed eleven-year-olds becoming millionaires from their own YouTube channels. I witnessed sixty-year-olds starting highly profitable side-hustles in network marketing after deciding that retirement wasn't for them. There was even a married couple making £20,000 a month by feeding each other Percy Pigs in their birthday suits, while eager fans paid to watch! I began to see possibilities for freedom and finances that my mind had never witnessed before.

What was this place where people were doing these extraordinary things, breaking the status quo and busting through anything deemed normal?

It was the *field of possibility*, where success beyond my wildest imagination lived. This was a different frequency and energetic field, which required a very different way of thinking. This field was where manifesting the crazy stuff belonged, and it required stepping away from a linear and predictable way of thinking and being.

The field of possibility

Playing on this field means showing up to life with a different set of rules where 'normal', 'realistic' and 'linear' simply do not apply. On this field, people are creating their dream lives with faith, waving goodbye to societal norms and banishing the idea of waiting till their sixties to get freedom. As I witnessed the possibility of this field, I felt myself being pulled from my predictable life: 'Noor, come here; come and leave the other field and try this one out!'

The rules on this field differ from the X = Y formulaic experience of the previous field. On this field we need to be able to say goodbye to predictability and hello to possibility. There is no linear time and space governing how quickly you can create success, and the rewards can be substantially greater. You are allowed to dream bigger than ever before, and the people on this field will support this, rather than feeling triggered. Picture this: you are in the supermarket doing your weekly grocery shop, and a woman with two children is standing at the front of the shop, shouting with joy, 'I've just made fifty thousand pounds a month for the last three months.' The shop is filled with everyday people who live on the field of predictability.

What do you feel the reaction to her would be by the majority of people in the supermarket? 'She's lying! She's crazy? She must be a drug dealer.'

Because this type of income makes absolutely no sense to most people, their reaction is *not* positive; it actually causes a negative reaction, as their predictable mind tries to grapple with these completely unpredictable results. It's akin to someone running onto a football pitch during a Premier League match and flashing their bits to everyone on live TV.

If you are used to living a controlled and predictable life and you've been taught how to create your own success through a linear and realistic mindset, you don't want anyone ruffling your feathers, especially if you've spent seven years educating yourself, are now in mountains of debt and are making less in a year than the mother at that supermarket makes in a month; or, even worse, less than the naked couple feeding each other Percy Pigs for £20,000 a month on OnlyFans.

Against all the mind-chatter and 'what ifs?', I did decide to take a giant step into the unknown and onto the unpredictable field of manifestation. But this field requires more courage to play bigger, more faith to be able to play in the unknown without your big, comfy security blanket. I was willing to do that, because the sounds of people living a life of freedom were too loud for me to ignore any longer.

However, most people will see the doorway to this life of possibility and will freak out. It's not their fault, as this is how the subconscious mind works against us, to try and keep us safe. As humans, we get deterred by uncertainty and by the fact that people around us will tell us it's not realistic. We feel we will be judged for trying to change, so we reluctantly retreat to where life feels safe. This is the subconscious mind stepping in and alerting us to the fact that the unknown is a potential threat, and to remain with the 'tribe' and the social norms of behaviour. The subconscious mind is primitive in nature and hasn't received the memo that venturing beyond the norm is okay, and that we are no longer living in tribes in caves, where disobedience of the rules means being sent away to fend for yourself.

This happened to me when I was looking to leave school to go to the BRIT performing-arts school at sixteen. For me, the BRIT School represented possibility, or what could be, but my parents urged me to stay in a more traditional school so that I could get good grades and attend university and, ultimately, have a back-up plan.

And so I listened to my parents and left my dream behind, to do what everyone else was doing. As people, we will unconsciously do what the majority do, because that's what feels most comfortable to the human mind. That's why if you choose to venture onto the field of possibility, it's important to understand that not everyone is going to get it, and that while it may be uncomfortable to think and act differently, you aren't going to get banished from the tribe!

There will be a minority of people on the predictable field who are ready for more, ready for new rules, and whose ears prick up. Instead of being negative, they will desire to know more and want to find out from the mother in the supermarket who made £50,000 a month how she did it. This is where someone begins to change their energetic field – they are willing to shift their mindset, expand their beliefs and push through predictable towards what is f*cking possible. It's a commitment to be a conscious creator in life, rather than simply exist.

This field has rules too, as defined by the VIA Manifesting Method®, which I'm going to outline for you in this part of the book. You need to learn to leave the field of predictability behind you, for the most part, if you wish to create your dream life. I want you to really harness your personal power and know, with every cell in your body, that you have the power to create the most incredible things by following the VIA Manifesting Method®. As you tune into a new frequency and mindset, you may even start to see miracles happen – or what I call 'What the fuck!' moments.

WTF moments

WTF moments are things that happen that seem impossible. They are things that we haven't actively taken action to manifest, and which spontaneously happen as though it's a miracle. This only occurs when we truly surrender and don't let any of our beliefs interfere. And these moments can happen to anyone. Let me share a story that exemplifies this in action.

For years one of my guilty pleasures was watching a very popular British reality-TV show. As I immersed myself in the predictable drama each week, I'd often have a strong desire to help some of the girls on the show. I just knew I could make a difference if I could have a conversation with them. It was not something that I was seriously considering or even thought possible! It was simply the purest of desires: I wanted to help those girls.

Months later I went to a party in London and two women walked up to me, and as my eyes focused through the copious number of Pornstar Martinis I'd drunk (way too quickly, in my excitement at a rare child-free night out) I noticed there was one of the girls from that exact reality-TV show. We started chatting, hit it off and a few months later she messaged me and asked me if I could coach her. What the fuck!

I began realizing this had happened many times in different forms, from small incidents of thinking about someone and then them calling out of the blue, to getting random private messages from celebrities asking to meet me (this has happened more than once). WTF moments can happen irrelevant of which field you reside on, because even when we live on the field of predictability we can still experience miracles – such as normal, everyday people winning the Lottery. But living life hoping for WTF moments to happen is unsustainable in the long term, and I'd much rather have a system that helps me reach all the possibilities I desire.

That's why in this book you are going to learn to play the rules of the field of possibility. And while you will visit the field of miracles and things will happen spontaneously out of thin air, your focus is on the field that you will actively function in. You aren't going to rely on spontaneous miracles, but will instead rely on meeting the universe halfway, to create what you desire. And it's important to note that, as humans, we will oscillate between the different energetic fields, but it's the field we choose to reside in the most, and the frequency we choose to experience the most, that will determine the result we create.

You are not a victim of your circumstances; you are not bound by the predictable steps that most people are living by; and you can take a quantum leap to your own success if you choose to.

Yes, it's a choice.

Choices are not always easy, but when you make the right ones, you can unlock a whole different playing field. Life is not a battle, it's a game, and what I'm about to share with you are the rules for playing it, so that you can win.

8.

V is for Vision

As a child, I'd often get told off for daydreaming at school. I'd lose myself in a make-believe world, where I had a little friend the size of my thumb who would hang out with me all day. While the likelihood of living out my Thumbelina fantasy was low, I also used to dream of being a children's author, performing on the stage of a West End musical or taking a leading role in a soap opera. I never dreamed of flying to the moon, nor did I have a desire to be a vet – because that simply wasn't part of my blueprint and thus of the vision that I had for my life.

Your vision for your life is aligned with your purpose, your values, your priorities and your deepest desires. Your biggest vision can often feel impractical and maybe even impossible, but don't be fooled. Your logical brain may interfere with tapping into this vision and will try to shut down anything that seems impractical, but the universe wants you to succeed and only codes in a vision that it is possible for you to bring to fruition, so do not doubt it!

As an adult, while I don't write children's books (yet!), I now get paid to write self-development books and teach thousands of people across the globe over social media, which is a bit like having my own TV show. That's because we only truly dream of things that are actually possible for us to manifest. If you've ever wondered how to manifest the life of your dreams and whether there is a secret ingredient that might help you, there is. It's understanding that your vision is like a mission that you can set out to accomplish. And what's the easiest way to accomplish this mission? Well, by living the life that is aligned to *you*.

Yep, that's it! Your purpose is to live your life in accordance with a vision that you'll be able to look back on and say, 'Yes, I lived a life that was true to me.' That means living the life you're meant to, becoming the person you're meant to be, fulfilling your highest potential and living with full-bodied purpose. That's what it means to be *you*.

The secret to becoming *you* is all about learning how to tune into your personal vision. Earlier on, I talked about our unique blueprint and how it's like a microchip placed inside you (see page 23). Your microchip was programmed with a custom vision for you – and only you – to fulfil. The universe is helpful and wants you to succeed, so it also gives you a map of the path to follow. You are destined for success, and all that it takes is for you to be yourself. And to reconnect and align with the real *you*.

Although the terms are often used interchangeably, your vision and your goals are different things. They're inextricably linked, but setting effective goals depends on having clear vision. Understanding the difference between goals and vision can help you ensure the maximum output in your life.

Remember: if you can daydream about something and that dream is fuelled with desire, then it means that you have the ability to manifest it.

It's through this vision that the universal intelligence is communicating what is possible for you. Your vision is the overarching umbrella for your whole life, beneath which goals hang off – imagine one of those big Australian hats with corks dangling off it! Your vision is the hat, and your goals are the corks. Your vision is the blueprint of your most epic life, and your goals are the stepping stones to get there.

Your goals help you bring your vision to life. They are the milestones that you hit in order to make your vision a reality and they produce results that you can use to measure your progress, while your vision is your desired overall result. Goals are the means to an end, while visions are the endpoints themselves. For example, if your vision is to be an international brand in the next five years, it's important to set monthly, quarterly or annual goals to help achieve that vision.

Your vision must also be dissected into the different pathways of your life. There is truly no point in having a vision for wealth if you don't also have a vision for your health, because there's no use having lots of money but being bed-bound with chronic illness. Equally, having a vision for your health but no vision for your relationships will hinder your success because, as humans, connection with others is important for our happiness. That's why every month in my programmes we meet to set our goals in eight different areas of our lives, to help bring our visions for life to fruition. These areas are:

1. Health/fitness
2. Love/romance
3. Personal growth/spiritual development
4. Charitable work/service
5. Friends/family
6. Career/business
7. Finance/wealth
8. Fun/hobbies/recreation.

Aligning with your vision boils down to a few fundamental points, starting with two important questions: What really matters to me? And if I could have anything I wanted, what would I wish for?

Before we dive into the three steps for curating your vision, I want you to take a moment and journal the following questions, allowing yourself to open up to the next-level version of yourself.

Coaching task: journal these questions

Write down in a journal your thoughts on the following questions:

- When you look back on your life on your deathbed, what do you know you want to have done and accomplished?
- What meaning do you want your life to have?
- What are the things you value?
- How do you want to feel?

Step one: Align

Often we believe that our vision is something we need to find or create out of thin air, but here's something amazing: your vision isn't something you need to think up all by yourself. Each of us has a purpose and, with that, a vision that matches it. We are inbuilt with a blueprint – we simply need to learn how to reconnect with it. First we must connect and *align* to the vision and *values* that are meant for us. Then we must *decide and declare* it non-negotiable, and finally we must *activate* our vision in the quantum field.

Have you ever thought you wanted to do something particular in life, but found yourself playing it down or telling others a different story? We do this because being honest about what we truly want is quite scary. That's why *aligning* to our vision starts with being as *honest* as you truly can be. Most of us don't like to admit what we really want, because it's safer to pretend that we don't desire exponential wealth, or a romantic partner, or a house bursting with kids, than be faced with the prospect that it might never happen.

That's why part of connecting and aligning to what we are meant to do with our lives, and creating that vision, is honesty – unadulterated, unabashed childlike honesty. Children are unfiltered and don't have the ability to contain their honesty. As we get older, we become aware of the status quo, worry about judgement and become protective of our emotions, and so without ever really realizing it, we become full-blown liars. But the person we are lying to most is ourselves. That's why honesty really is the best policy if you wish to create the life you dream of. We stay small because we continually lie to ourselves, as a defence mechanism, but vulnerability and openness about what we want form the powerful message that we need to send to the universe.

Think back to when you were a child, writing a list to Santa. You wrote everything down – no holding back. You weren't worried that Santa wouldn't bring it, or worried whether what you wanted was even made at the North Pole workshop; you wrote it down in the full belief that it was yours. Channelling that same honesty about what you want, and don't want, in your life is important, because you need a clean energetic field of energy for the universe to work with.

Coaching task: plan your vision

Download the vision planner at www.thisisyourdream.com/success and start mapping out the vision for each of those eight areas of your life, creating your very own Santa's list for the universe!

However, there is a problem many of us encounter when trying to reconnect with what we really want – we forget what we actually desire when we operate as a humanoid, because we get so caught up in surviving life that it's hard to think about what we wish to thrive in life. For that reason, if you feel stuck about what you *do* want, start with what you *don't* want.

Coaching task: specify your dislikes

Write down a list of areas in your current life that you are not happy with. This will serve as the springboard of data from which you will create change:

- I don't want to be overweight.
- I don't want to be single.
- I don't want to have more month than money.
- I don't want to be in a nine-to-five job.
- I don't want to have to say 'yes' to going to the knitting club with Julie every Thursday.

Whatever it is, write it down. Next, take this list and flip it, by writing what the opposite of these dislikes looks like. Now you've gone from 'not this' to 'this'.

The second part of aligning is truly creating clarity around what you value. Let me share a story with you that will show you why our values are so crucial when it comes to the vision for our life.

When I was seven years old I desperately wanted one of those troll toys – the ones with bright-pink hair with a gem in their tummy, because they were limited-edition ones that you could *wish* on. Yep, the TV advert told me that if I got one of those, it would be like my own personal genie. The problem was that my mum said I couldn't have one because they were a waste of money.

One day after school we were walking through the local shopping centre with our au pair and we stopped at Clintons Cards. That's when I caught a glimpse of the troll's pink fluffy hair and glistening purple gem. Oh, it was the beautiful wish-fulfilling troll. I made a terrible decision at that moment – I wanted that troll so badly that I picked it up and stuffed it in my school bag. I knew I'd done something wrong, but I really wanted it, so I stole it.

When I got home our au pair found it in my school bag and told my dad, who was quite rightly angry and disappointed. The next day I was frogmarched back to the shop, where I handed back the pink-haired troll to a bewildered shop assistant. I remember that day so vividly. The shame, the guilt and the fear were etched on my mind.

As I grew up there were many more incidents where I wanted things I couldn't have, and I know that was a huge subconscious driver for me to create the life I have now. Being successful for me is the freedom to be who I want to be, do what I wish and have what I desire, without having to beg, borrow or steal. In fact last year I was working with my own coach and the whole troll-related fiasco came up in a session, and as part of the healing process I needed to forgive myself for stealing the troll. Yes, I gave it back, but I still carried the shame of doing so, all these years later. After that powerful session I went on eBay to see if I could find one of those trolls and, lo and behold, I saw one onscreen with the pink hair and purple gem and purchased it immediately. My inner child lit up, and while I paid three times the original amount for one, decades later, I finally got my wishing troll. This marked true success for me, because of the freedom I have to make my own choices and buy what I want. Freedom is by far one of my most-core values.

Next I want you to think about what you *value*. Values are the foundation of our vision. Imagine that Australian hat again. Values form the rim of the hat beneath the crown. They are basic and fundamental beliefs that guide or motivate our attitudes or actions. They help us to determine what is important to us. Values describe the personal qualities that we choose to embody in order to guide our actions; the sort of person we want to be; the manner in which we treat both ourselves and others. They create the foundations on which your vision can stand tall.

Coaching note: what do you really value in life?

I want you to think about what you truly value – what matters to you. At www.thisisyourdream.com/success I've included a values-finder list, to help you become clear on that. When you know what you value, you can use this as a guiding tool for everything you do in life.

The kind of success you desire should be underpinned by what *truly matters* to you and is *personal* to you. When you get your vision and values in alignment, it's so much easier to send out a clean and effective message to the universe about what you need it to deliver. Because my values are freedom and family, if I started a business that meant working eighty hours a week and having to spend time away from my kids, there would be a conflict between what I desired and the reality of the situation. The last part of aligning is allowing yourself to tune into what you really desire.

Coaching task: write down your desires

Get a piece of paper or your journal and find a quiet place to sit and write. Before you begin, take three deep breaths and ask the universe to guide you through this exercise. What do you truly desire in your life? What would you regret not having done, if you were told this was your last day? What do you dream of doing? Be honest and get this all down on paper.

Step two: Decide and declare

Once you've specified what you want, what you don't want, what you value and what you truly desire, it's time to *decide and declare*. How many times have you said, 'I'd like [insert whatever you want]' or 'I hope it works out' or 'I wish that would happen'? When we become clear on our dreams and what it is that we wish to create in life, there is an important next step. We need to make a non-negotiable, full-body decision to make it happen. Think of a time in your life when you really wanted something done and put your mind to it, and it paid off. Just feel the energy concerning how you felt – not only when you decided, but also once you had accomplished that thing. It's a very different experience from when we hope and wish for something.

There's no point in simply hoping and wishing, when you can make a *decision*. Say out loud three times, 'I decide to have [insert your vision].' Whatever it is, say that you decide on it, declare it out loud and feel the energy that pulses through your body.

If we were plugged into a machine that could decipher our frequency when we decide something positive, it would be vibrating at a much higher frequency. Decisions permeate our very being, activating parts of our brains that help us to stay motivated. When I decided to make my business a success, there was no Plan B and there was a definite focus of my energy on one endpoint. A decision involves a very different energy from hoping or wishing.

By deciding what we want, we are pushing out a thought into the universal substance, through which everything is created and manifested into physical reality. When we decide we want something, we also get another ingredient thrown into the manifesting mix – expectancy.

Imagine that you are sitting at a table in your favourite restaurant. The waiter comes and you know with certainty what you wish to order. You know it because you *love* that dish and desire it. You can almost taste it already and are excited for its arrival, as you hear your tummy rumble. Your waiter takes your order and then brings you a glass of wine to enjoy while your meal is prepared. As you sit sipping your wine and chatting to your friends, you are in happy anticipation of the delicious meal (excitement), but you aren't worried that it won't arrive (expectancy). You decided what you wanted because you desired it, and you *know* it's being made and have utter faith that it will be delivered to your table shortly. You enjoy the interim. You don't sit there fretting and worrying that your dish won't arrive.

Can you imagine if every time you went out for food, you insisted to the waiter that you should be allowed to watch it being prepared in the kitchen because you didn't believe it was being cooked? Imagine standing over the chefs, quizzing their every move and nagging them to hurry up, because you want your meal now. You'd probably soon have nowhere to go out and eat! You'd be the crazy person blacklisted from every eatery!

We have faith in the service because that's what restaurants do. If we can execute that same level of expectancy in the universe, knowing that there is a time for preparation, we can learn to enjoy the space in between. Everything in the world needs time to gestate. That is a universal law. The universe needs time to bring to fruition what you desire, and that's why expectancy is important, as it allows you to enjoy the period during which your desire is gestating and coming to fruition.

Expectancy shows faith, and faith is often the missing ingredient when people are trying to manifest. If they cannot physically see their meal being cooked by the chef, they do not believe it is being cooked. We need to trust that there is magic happening behind the scenes and that the universe is cooking up a storm, even when we cannot see it.

There is one more important thing to note here: a decision met with desire is a force to be reckoned with. We desire things that we want, not things that we need. This is a powerful distinction. We cannot manifest the things we need with as much ease as the things we desire, because need is fuelled by fear. A desire is pure because we simply want it.

You see, our vision is not usually something we *need* – it's rooted in a desire for what we want and what is possible for us. If you are trying to create your dream life out of the energy of 'need', this represents lack, and the energy of 'lack' is not a creative force or the frequency for manifesting what we want. Need comes from fear, and fear is the opposing energetic force to creating magic. So it's really important to recognize that your vision is bigger than 'What do I *need* to survive?' and is more about 'What *could* I create if I remembered how powerful I was?' and 'What do I truly *desire* in my life?'

I desired a book deal, but I didn't *need* one. I desired to build a house, but I didn't *need* to build it. I dreamed of having a business, but I didn't *need* one. I desired to make £10,000 a month, but no one needs that to survive.

The best desires are something you want, not something you need. Desire makes your decision so much more potent. If you can be clear about *why* you want something and what feeling it will give you, then you put yourself in a powerful position for creation and for manifesting a life better than your dreams.

Coaching task: dig deep

Think about what you've written down on your very own Santa list to the universe. Next to it, I want you to infuse some desire by asking yourself these questions:

- Why will it be of greater good to my life?
- Why will it be of greater good to the life of those closest to me?
- How will it affect those further away from me?

Dig deep to think about this. Sometimes we want things just because we want them, but I want you to practise digging a little deeper, because everything we desire has a reason attached to it. There's always a feeling that we're trying to chase. Understanding those feelings is incredibly important for making sure that the third part of this sequence works exceptionally well.

You can have it all

There's another crucial component in creating and aligning with your vision that I want to address. As a society, and particularly for women, there's a destructive underlying story that weaves its way through our lives, and it needs to be addressed if you wish to create exponential success in all areas of your life.

There is an urban myth rolling around that we cannot create success across the board, and that somehow we must be okay with sacrificing one part of our lives for another part. You can't possibly have a toned body, financial freedom, a loving relationship, be a great parent and have brilliant friends. We tend to believe that there's no such thing in the real world as someone who *has it all*. This is a belief that I need you to quash quicker than Usain Bolt doing a sprint.

Don't get me wrong: there are plenty of people on social media portraying their perfectly filtered lives, when behind the scenes is in fact a shit-show. They are not the people I want you to look to. We can do all the things we desire that are important to us and in alignment with our values. You can have it *all*. You don't need to sacrifice your career for motherhood, or your friends for your relationship, or your health for money. We can all strive to have a healthy body, great friends, a loving relationship (if you want one) and a vocation that pays us really well. It's truly possible to feel successful in all areas of your life – remember that success is decided by *you*.

When you try to keep up with the Joneses or the Kardashians, you actually can't have it all, because you're motivated by a comparison that somehow you aren't good enough. Also, you do not need to have it all right now. But when you commit to having everything you desire, you commit to bettering yourself – not in comparison to others, but in comparison only to yourself.

Many people that I speak to don't actually think this is possible. Why? Because we don't have many role models in our lives that show this. And remember that we are products of our upbringing. Think of the media images we consume, such as those in TV shows and movies. It's not that usual to see a financially successful woman who is also a great mother and in great shape, with amazing friendships. I mean it just wouldn't make for good TV!

So we see rich dysfunctional people, or successful women who are unlucky in love, or people in love who struggle with children or money – and when the narrative is that you can't have it all, we buy into that belief. We believe that somehow if we make one area of our lives epic, we must take from another area. When it comes to vision and goal-setting, most people become fixated on *one* area and this is a fundamental flaw. We make this choice to work on one part of our lives and then wonder why other parts suffer.

- Decide you can have success in all areas of your life.
- Decide what that looks like and why it's important to you.
- Decide *now* that you are going to live the life you were meant to live.
- Decide *now* that you're going to live the life that is truly yours.
- Decide *now* that you're not going to leave this lifetime without having fulfilled your unique purpose.
- Decide *now* that you're not going to look back with regret.

Recognize that no one's life is perfect, and your life hasn't been given to you so that you can spend it curating an image of perfection to the outside world on social media. It's okay to be real!

You do not have to sacrifice one part of your life for another, as long as you know what you need to do and how to take the right action to make the change you desire. Which brings me nicely to the next step: activate.

Step three: Activate

The last piece of the puzzle is that once you have a clear vision and have decided what you want, it's time to *activate* it in the quantum field. 'The quantum thingamajiggy?' you might say.

As humans, we live in a 3D world governed by linear time and space as perceived by our five senses. This is the reality with which our physical body identifies, but it is far from the whole picture. This is the reality in which most people live: 'I only believe what I can see, hear, taste, touch and smell – that is *real* life.' The habit of seeing only that which our five senses permit renders us totally blind to what we might otherwise see.

Considering that our eyes are limited to seeing less than 1 per cent of the electromagnetic spectrum, which is the only portion visible to the human eye, it's conceivable that perhaps there is another plane we can access to create what we desire. In order to cultivate the skill of seeing the invisible, we need to consciously and deliberately disentangle our minds from the evidence brought to our brains by our senses. We need to intentionally focus our energy on a different field of energy, which the late mystic and author Neville Goddard described as 'thinking fourth-dimensionally'.

When you close your eyes and begin to focus, you enter this realm of thinking fourth-dimensionally, which is a space of nothing that is referred to as the 'quantum field'. This is the space of incredible creation. According to the researcher and educator Dr Joe Dispenza in his blog, the definition of the quantum field is 'an invisible field of frequency or energy [or you could say a field of intelligence or consciousness] that connects everything physical and material. It is this field of pure energy, which exists beyond our senses, that gives form to this three-dimensional reality.'

The quantum field is the space where anything is possible. In the quantum field, your thoughts and corresponding emotions create your reality. When I first heard about this, I wanted a VIP backstage pass to get me to the quantum field asap, so that I could be making myself some dream life. So how do we access this quantum field of possibility, where you consciously create your reality?

If you can get into the habit of withdrawing attention from the region of sensation and concentrating it on the invisible, you are then able to penetrate beyond the world of the senses to see that which is invisible. Close your eyes and focus with clear intent on whatever you wish to create in your life. We have been given the incredible tool of imagination, as humans; we are the only species to have this, and the reason is so that we can create our lives in this space. When we can enter this space and see what we desire as though it is already done in the quantum field, then we can then go into our 3D lives again with the assumption that it's already achieved. This is what the author and mystic Neville Goddard called the 'law of assumption'. As soon as we assume the feelings of our desires as though they are already fulfilled, our higher self finds ways for their attainment and discovers all the methods for their realization.

Neville Goddard said, 'I know of no clearer definition of the means by which we realize our desires than to experience in imagination what we would experience in the flesh, were we to achieve our goal. This imaginary experience of the end with acceptance, wills the means.' This basically means that when we can see in our minds the desire being manifested, then the *how* will find the way to manifest it.

So I want you to close your eyes and spend a few moments visualizing a scene that represents what you want to manifest having already manifested. Bring all your senses to the scene and, most importantly, feel how you would feel if it is already done. This helps you to assume the feeling that the universe has already delivered what you desire.

Coaching note: summary

1. *Align* with your vision and *values* for your life.
2. *Decide* they are yours by *declaring* them out loud and writing them down. Sense how that decision feels in your body.
3. *Activate* it in the quantum field by closing your eyes and seeing the vision of your life, really bringing in all the senses to create a vivid mental picture.

Okay, so now that you have aligned with your values, decided and activated, you can set goals that will help make that vision a reality.

This breaks down your vision for your life into milestones that you wish to achieve, seeing them like projects. This may feel like an overwhelming task at first, but there are a few simple steps to follow.

Coaching task: what/why/when/how?

1. Break your goals down into different projects of your life, such as health, wealth and relationships, so that you can see the ultimate outcome for each area. This is the *what* done.
2. Now ask yourself *why* each of these desired projects matters to you.
3. Think about *when* you would love to celebrate them by.
4. Next ask yourself *how* you will go about getting there.
5. Last but not least, I want you to think about everything you need to learn/know/ask in order to get there. *What do you need to do or acquire?*

Perhaps you will need mentorship or coaching? Maybe you need to up-level your skills or knowledge. This is where you figure out your blind spots and think about who can support you in filling them in. What help do you need? What tools or resources do you require? When you can become aware of the obstacles, you can seek to overcome them.

9.

I is for Identity

The phrase 'your personality becomes your personal reality' was running around my head like a toddler who had eaten too much sugar. Since I was twenty-nine I had become mildly obsessed with personally developing myself, and one thing that became abundantly clear to me was that in order to get to the vision of the life I wanted, I would need to change who I was.

And when I say 'change who I was' I don't mean change who I *am* at my core, but who I'd *become* as a result of years of conditioning. Changing who I was didn't mean that I needed to try and 'put on a new persona' or be inauthentic; quite the opposite: it meant stripping back all the bullshit and tapping into the real *me*. Instead of the mental story that was keeping me stuck, I needed a new story and new thoughts, because after years of self-development and becoming a coach, it was clear that my thoughts were creating my life. You see, our thoughts create emotions, emotions drive our behaviours, and our behaviours create the results we see.

But what lies behind our thoughts – those automatic pings of energetic information that pop into our head? Well, our beliefs, which are the stories we have created about who we are, and all the decisions that we have made about life since childhood.

My spiritual self had big dreams and held the key to all the abundance I desired. My soul knew what I was capable of and how to get there, but if my beliefs were in conflict with this, then I would also feel like getting to my dreams was kind of like taking one step forward and two steps back. This is why we unconsciously self-sabotage. Until I got my beliefs in line with my desires, and my human self and my spiritual self working together, I'd always end up unconsciously repelling what I desired because the ego is louder and we trust its voice more. This is what the self-help experts meant when they talked about 'alignment' – it's having conscious desires and subconscious beliefs in line with one another, and our ego and soul being in cahoots, rather than in a battle.

Your life is a result of everything you think about. To be honest, your flesh, bones and muscles can be reduced to 70 per cent water and a few chemicals of little value, but it is your mind and what you think about that make *you* who you truly are and what you are capable of achieving in life. Thoughts are behind all discoveries, all inventions, all achievement; conversely, they are also the reason there is a huge shelf in the universal field with most of the human population's dreams neatly stacked upon it, getting dustier by the minute.

That's why the secret to success lies not outside us, but within the thoughts of each and every one of us. We need to shed the beliefs that are holding us back, the attitudes that are keeping us stuck, and realign with our own values, not the values that were bestowed upon us as children.

As I explained earlier in the book (see page 41), our subconscious mind is the one running the show. The conscious mind likes to think it is in control, but anyone who has ever studied the workings of the brain knows better. It is hypothesized that the subconscious is responsible for 95 per cent of what we do on a daily basis – *95 freaking per cent*! And yet we beat ourselves up when we set goals and stay positive and wonder why they do not come to fruition. We are really fighting against the odds, when we expect to create radical change in our lives using only 5 per cent of our mental faculties.

I want to share a story with you now that I'm sure many of you readers will resonate with.

Every so often I love to treat myself to a facial, and on a chilly November morning I had booked myself in for some much-needed TLC. I was lying down having my face pricked with a stamp containing twenty titanium needles. The needles would prick my skin, allowing a mix of vitamins and minerals to penetrate below the surface.

As each tiny prick went in, I got to talking to my lovely facialist, who told me that she had started her own little business, but every time she went to post something about her business or promote it, she would hear a voice in her head attempting to talk her out of it. She would then put off whatever task she had set out to do and would eventually find herself back at square one. Raise your hand if you've ever experienced the same thing?

'Ah!' I said, while she placed the red LED lamp over my face for the second phase of making my face look wow-worthy. 'The good old shitty committee has come out to play,' I told her.

She laughed. 'Yes!'

'The shitty committee always shows up when we are trying to venture into new, greener pastures,' I explained to her. 'That's its job.'

The shitty committee is the voice of the ego, the collective voice of our parents, the media and society, plus the stories we have accumulated from childhood about ourselves – like that really untactful family member who not-so-subtly points out that you've put on a few pounds and blurts out, 'My dear, you've got fat!' The shitty committee has no tact and will turn up uninvited to every party, giving its unsolicited negative advice. This leaves you feeling exposed and vulnerable and so you retreat – because it is the voice of reason, surely? It must be the voice of truth.

Well, no. Such thoughts are an automatic response to the data that your mind has processed. As we discussed earlier, the mind wants to keep us safe, and any sort of perceived threat rings alarm bells in our bodies. It's filtered through the mind's database and is searched to match it with relevant sources. And if there's any chance that this experience could potentially put us in an 'unsafe' situation, the shitty committee will pop up. It is there to keep us safe and to dissuade us from taking the leaps necessary in life for us to change. It is the 'Oh, but . . .' that follows the desire and it's not there to be polite, it's there to blunt.

'So what happens when you try to post on social media to promote your business?' I asked my facialist.

Her reply was one that I've now heard probably thousands of times, from incredible humans right across the world. 'I second-guess myself. I compare myself to everyone else out there, who is amazing at doing what I do, and then I don't feel good enough and so I stop.'

And there it is. The golden nugget of information that I was looking for. The story that she believed about herself; the same story that almost every incredible and capable person I've ever worked with has brought to the table. My facialist had a destructive story about herself that somehow she was not good enough. Good enough compared to what? To whom? That is the question of all questions, which we need to unravel right now.

What it is important to notice here is that it was *simply a thought* (or a few thoughts) that were creating a huge barrier between this lovely lady and her dreams – once again showing us the sheer power of thoughts in creating our lives. As we've already seen, that thought has the power to set my facialist's nervous system into action, in response to the perceived threat of posting on social media, and then she ends up getting stuck in fight-or-flight mode. When we realize that there cannot be any emotion, or any reaction, without the generating force of thoughts behind it, we can start to see why changing our story is so incredibly powerful.

I went on to tell her that the statistics concerning how many businesses fail within a few years are shockingly high. 'Why?' you might ask. Well, it's not down to lack of strategy or information. There is no lack of either of those in the world we live in – a quick Google search and you can find the steps to building most businesses online. However, if strategy was the only thing that made anyone successful, then following steps one to ten on how to lose weight, or how to make money, or how to make a baby, would work every time for every person. However, strategy is the 5 per cent conscious activity fighting against the hidden 95 per cent force below the surface.

'Okay,' she said. 'What do I do?'

I asked her what the purpose was of using needles to stamp my face before putting on the vitamin mixture.

'Well, as we puncture the layer of the skin, all the goodness can penetrate lower and can do its magic. Otherwise, it's only super-ficial and won't get you the result you desire,' she replied

'Boom!' I said.

It's the same with us humans. Most of us try to change our lives on a superficial level; we repeat affirmations, write gratitude lists and loudly affirm what we desire, but we don't penetrate below the layer of our consciousness into our subconscious, where our iden-tity lies, where the 95 per cent of who we are is lurking, plus all the stories that we hold about ourselves.

In that 95 per cent lies our *identity*. In psychology, the term 'iden-tity' is commonly used to describe the distinctive qualities or traits that make each of us individual humans unique. Identities are strongly associated with self-concept, self-image (one's mental model of oneself), self-esteem and individuality. Personality traits, abilities, likes and dislikes, your belief system or moral code and the things that motivate you – all of these contribute to your self-image or your unique identity as a person. Unless we nourish that 95 per cent in the same way the facial was nourishing the lower layer of my skin (hopefully making me look less sleep-deprived and more yummy mummy), we will not get a long-lasting result.

Coaching note: the shitty committee

I want you to take a moment to think about all the stories that come up for you when you try to embark on something new. What are the recurring negative thoughts that the shitty committee is telling you? Awareness is key.

The shadow self

So how do these stories get created? Between the ages of two and eight, everything we hear, see and experience soaks into us like that sponge I talked about earlier (see page 39). Some of those encounters will imprint on our minds if they have significant meanings or high emotions attached. My facialist will have experienced something that resulted in her creating a story about herself – a debilitating belief that made her feel that she was worth less than others. The trigger may have been something seemingly trivial or innocent, like not getting picked for a part in a school play, or it could have been something more traumatic, such as being bullied, but somewhere along the line there was a little girl who decided she wasn't good enough.

This then created the subconscious script 'I'm not good enough' and, like a tab left open on your computer, that script continued to run in the background of everything she did, embedded in the core part of her identity and following her around like a shadow she couldn't shake off.

We all have a shadow self. This refers to parts of yourself – whether personality traits, emotions or thoughts – that are difficult to accept. It was the famed psychoanalyst Carl Jung who popularized the idea of the shadow self. We all come into the world open and free of judgement, but as we get older we have experiences that cause us to judge ourselves. No one wants to accept that they are not good enough, but through our conversation I managed to bring awareness to my facialist, as I have to the thousands of incredible human beings that I get to work with. Awareness can lead to understanding, which can lead to healing.

I want you to imagine life as a big movie for a moment. When we get cast in the roles for the movie of our lives, we are each allocated a brief about our character, which includes traits and attributes. These are things like our age, our gender at birth, our place of birth and the physical characteristics that we have no control over. Then, as we start participating in the role, we get to choose other traits, such as our occupation, our political affiliation, our hobbies and the place where we live.

The core part of our identity represents just one level – the level of our traits, values, attitudes and beliefs that make us who we are and how we operate and act in the movie of our life. For example, our beliefs about money, our values concerning what is important to us, our attitudes towards relationships and food, and the way we behave around certain people.

While we may think our identity is something cultivated after we are born, the opposite is true. Our identity is influenced long before we are even conceived. The fact is that our society – regardless of the customs or cultures within it – has already begun shaping our identity through years of categorization and labelling, based on traits and expected behaviours. Before we're born, these predetermined groups are already created. For instance, if you are a woman born in Saudi Arabia, your identity as a woman will be vastly different from that of a woman born in the UK.

Of course on top of the influences of society, our families and loved ones have a significant impact on who we become. As they are the first people we are exposed to, we consciously and subconsciously look to our parents, older siblings and extended family members for the building blocks of our identity formation; and throughout our formative years, our subconscious mind is that sponge soaking up everything, creating the scripts and stories that we will live by.

Once a belief or idea has been accepted by the subconscious mind as a child and forms a script, it remains our story until it is replaced by another story: a belief or idea. The longer a story is held, the more it tends to become a fixed habit or thought pattern. This is how habits of action are formed – both good and bad ones. An ingrained habit then forms a pattern that acts like a printed circuit, which is followed faithfully whenever the pattern gets triggered. Habits are scripts that we, as actors in our movie, will follow automatically.

For the most part, our lives are the same on a day-to-day basis and we unconsciously get through life, like most humanoids. We wake up in the same bed, follow similar morning routines, work with the same people, have the same conversations with our family, and we rinse and repeat this. We think the same stuff, feel the same stuff and tend to behave the same way on a daily basis, which is why our results (the movie of our lives) are always the same, and the end of the movie is really predictable. The conclusion of our movie will be determined by these scripts.

For most people, the 95 per cent that lurks in their subconscious will run the show, holding them hostage to their current life because they are none the wiser. When we try to change our lives from the same version of ourselves that we are today, we unwittingly invite the shitty committee to come in and block us. It can become a mental block that can feel so debilitating it causes us to physically stop – just as my lovely facialist discovered.

Subconscious Rescripting®

We need to be bigger than the shitty committee, we need to be stronger than the shitty committee – we need a new identity that's bigger than the previous version of ourselves. It's like having a spiritual facelift. By accessing the subconscious and changing your scripts – which you can do – you can get your stories and desires in cohesion working towards your vision, not against it.

We all need thoughts of success running through our veins, rather than the noise of the shitty committee trying to talk us out of doing the things we need to do in order to change our lives. I had been a slave to the shitty committee for years, decades even.

One of the important rules of the subconscious mind is that what is expected tends to be realized, because the subconscious mind works 24/7 to make sure you are right. As the Greek philosopher Aristotle appropriately observed, 'We become what we think about.' If we do not think we are good enough to succeed, then we will never be good enough to succeed.

So when we step out to create success, we have to understand that wanting to create success is our dream, but our dream is only as strong as the scripts it is built upon. Our personal reality is a result of our personality, and who we believe we are and what we believe we are capable of. What I've discovered, after working with thousands of people, is that what appears to be self-sabotage is really just a misalignment between external conscious desires and internal subconscious scripts. The answer is not to change your external desires (though after years of struggling, that is exactly what many people do); the answer is to update old subconscious programmes and stories so that they align with conscious desires – I call this Subconscious Rescripting®. We need to create stories in our minds that help propel us forward, not hold us back. So instead of the shitty committee showing up uninvited, we are able to override it and start to have beliefs and thoughts that are conducive to our success. That means we need to take our 5 per cent and use it to change the 95 per cent – yes, that's a task and requires discipline, but it can be done, because I've seen not only my life change rapidly due to it, but also the lives of many people that I care about.

When we rewrite the script, we play a role in our lives that can lead to a happy ending, not the ending that we assumed it would lead to, based on what we have seen or been modelled by. We get to harness the power of neuroplasticity to re-create version 2.0 of ourselves. The reason this is important is that through neuroplasticity the brain is consistently rewiring itself and modifying its connections. We can use this to relearn new ways of being.

So how did it end with my facialist? I explained to her that she would need to start changing her mindset and thought patterns. She needed to *become* a successful person by embedding into the subconscious mind scripts that would help her achieve her goals of being a successful businesswoman. And whichever belief her subconscious mind believed to be true was the one it would fixate on, because opposing beliefs cannot be held at the same time.

If I asked you to think two thoughts at the same time, you would find it impossible. It's like if I said to look at two sides of a coin at the same time – you could not. So the stronger thought that you focus on will dominate the outcome in your life. The subconscious mind seeks congruence, so when opposing ideas are presented, it can accept only one of them. This is why there are so many battles and outright wars over belief systems. When an individual buys into a particular belief, he or she seeks to create alliances with others who hold a congruent belief, and to avoid those who don't. This is why many people will struggle to step out and do big things when they are surrounded by people who are not on the same journey. We will cover this in more detail later on.

So to enjoy true success and make sure we can manifest what we desire with ease, we need to create new scripts that we can live our lives by, so that the ending of our movie is one we can be proud of. But what if you don't believe the stories you tell yourself? Well, you gotta fake it till you make it. This does not mean being a fake person; it means that you have got to embody the successful version of yourself way before the physical world shows you evidence of it.

Coaching note: get up close and personal

It's time to get really up close and personal with your own stories. Think about something you are trying to achieve – a goal you are wanting to manifest. Ask yourself, 'What recurring thoughts come up when I think about this thing?' List every negative thought that occurs to you. This will give you insights into your stories that you need to change.

Now that you have awareness of your current subconscious stories and scripts, it's time to harness the power of neuroplasticity and begin to shift your identities and beliefs so that you are in alignment with what you desire.

10.

*Change the f*cking story*

One of the greatest discoveries from the field of neuroplasticity is that we can change who we are. Many of us learned in school that, once we become adults, the brain is static and rigid. Until only a few decades ago, science led us to believe that we were doomed to our genetics and conditioning, and that the saying 'Old dogs can't learn new tricks' was the reality that we were governed by. Now it's understood that the brain's neuroplasticity enables it to reorganize pathways, create new connections and, in some cases, even create new neurons.

At birth, every nerve cell or neuron in the cerebral cortex has an estimated 2,500 synapses, or small gaps between the neurons where nerve impulses are relayed. By the age of three, this number has grown to a massive 15,000 synapses per neuron. However, the average adult has only about half that number because, as we gain new experiences, some connections are strengthened while others are eliminated. This process is known as *synaptic pruning*. By developing new connections and pruning away weak ones, the brain can adapt to the changing environment.

So how can we become the person we want to be, before we *are* actually the person we want to be? By understanding that we can create new neural pathways through repetition – and while it may not feel real to begin with – as we keep getting those new neurons to fire, we start to rewire the mind and create new stories that are conducive to our success, not just at a non-tangible level, but within our actual brains.

When it comes to truly mastering our identity, we get to choose who we want to be. Yes, we have a choice. We get to choose our beliefs, what we value, and we do it on our own terms and in accordance with what we want as individuals, not what we think we should want because it makes our parents happy or conforms to general norms. By *choosing who we want to be*, we are empowering ourselves energetically to move towards our dreams. This is the first phase of Subconscious Rescripting®.

You are the writer of your own script, and this is your chance to start creating a story that feels exciting, and crafting a destiny that is in alignment. One of the greatest writers on manifestation, Neville Goddard, spoke about the 'law of assumption' as a vehicle to doing this (see page 80). The law of assumption is different from the law of attraction, because the latter is a law of the universe, whereas the former is a law that we should live by if we want the universal law of attraction to work in our favour.

Whether you like it or not, you are constantly either attracting into your life or repelling what you desire, because whatever energy you are giving out, the universe will match it. The law of assumption suggests that what we assume to be true is what we will eventually manifest. Goddard stated that our assumptions about life have immense power to positively or negatively impact the fulfilment of our wishes and desires.

The definition of the word 'assumption' is 'a thing that is accepted as true or as certain to happen, without proof'. Therefore the law of assumption takes a reverse approach to working towards a goal. Most people believe they will be a certain way once their goals are met, but this law states that if we act and feel as if our desires have already come to fruition, they will manifest. In simple terms, the law of assumption proposes that *what we assume to be true will actually come true*. This isn't about being a fake person or inauthentic; this is about living our spiritual truth before it's a physical reality – it's about stepping into the future version of yourself, knowing that if you have vision for your life and desires in your heart, then they are meant for you.

Part of assuming that something is happening is really thinking about the beliefs, ideas and feelings that you would have if the spiritual truth was also now a physical truth. If what you wanted had manifested, what would you be thinking, how would you be feeling and what would you be doing?

Harnessing the power of neuroplasticity

When I began the journey of getting my first book deal, I did something that most people would have seen as a bit bonkers. As I was getting rejection after rejection (yep, book deals are a tough gig), I grabbed my phone, went onto Facebook and started writing out a post. I began writing about how unbelievably excited I was to be sharing that I had got my first book deal, and thanks to all the people who had helped me get there. And as I worked, I felt the rush of emotion: 'It will happen one day.' I was writing this post in the full assumption that I would get a book deal. You see, by harnessing the power of neuroplasticity, we can rescript our stories and input new scripts that form stories that are conducive to our success.

I didn't post the post, but I copied it into my notes and every day I would read it, allowing myself to sense the excitement of how it would feel. I was choosing the identity of a published author; I was thinking about where I'd have my book-launch party; I planned how I would market my book to my audience. It hadn't happened yet in the physical world, but in my heart and my soul it was *real*. Around six months after I wrote that post I got to post it for real, and it was a magical moment of proof that assuming the end result before it actually happened was incredibly powerful. Consider this:

- We can choose to be the person who thinks negative thoughts about the fulfilment of what we want, or we can choose to have positive thoughts.

- We can choose to be lazy about taking the action required to manifest what we want, or we can choose to be productive.
- We can choose to be the victim in our life story, or we can choose to be the hero.
- It truly is a choice.

Neuroplasticity affords us the privilege to change our actions and modify our behaviour, our thought processes and our personality to produce outcomes that are more desirable. When we have new thoughts, we can create new neural pathways, and the more we practise these thoughts, take action and assume the identity of being that person, the more embedded in our minds they become. And since our thoughts have an impact on our emotions, which affect our energy, we can become a magnet for what we desire. This is why Subconscious Rescripting® is so powerful. It enables us to bypass the critical factors of the conscious mind and the shitty committee, and the subconscious mind creates new stories of who we want to be. The way we bypass the critical mind is by communing with the subconscious mind when it's in an alpha or theta brainwave state, which is essentially a state of relaxation. We can communicate with the subconscious mind that it's safe to close the tab down on the previous day's events, which keeps us an emotional hostage to the past, and so we can focus on moving forward and reprogramming the mind for the future beliefs we want to have.

But it's still a choice to consciously change our mind. We need to use the 5 per cent to change the 95 per cent. It takes discipline at the beginning to override decades of conditioning that have made us the person we are today. It takes courage to decide *not* to be a victim and to step out of our comfort zone. It takes consistent action to reprogram our mind. And it takes faith to assume that something is already fulfilled when it isn't. But I know that you if truly want an extraordinary life, you can do these things.

Act like the person you want to become. When you do this, your brain sees you taking this action and changes the way it relates to you. When your brain starts to see you high-fiving yourself in the mirror and rooting for yourself, it says, 'Oh, wow, Noor loves herself! She's caring for herself. We don't need to beat Noor up.' Choosing a new identity means choosing to love yourself and have beliefs that support you, not beliefs that you are not good enough.

You can commit – I believe in you. You can be brave and show up for those big dreams. Because what's the other option? Stay in the field of predictability with the masses, always wondering, 'What if?'

I definitely didn't want that life, so I'm helping you work on creating a positive identity so that you know it's supporting you in making your dream life a reality. And then you need to take action – non-negotiable action.

Can I hear an 'Amen'?

Earlier in the book I talked about the first phase of Subconscious Rescripting®. Don't worry, I won't leave you hanging, but will be covering this in greater depth in the final part of the book. But before that, let's get stuck into the next step of the VIA Manifesting Method®. Now it's time to get your ass in gear and take some action!

A is for Action

I stood at the top of the big blue waterslide while on holiday in Egypt. My heart was racing and I had my eyes fixed on Richard and my daughters, who were waving rapidly at me from down below while shouting '*Go*, Mummy!' Even though I was at the front of the queue, I kept letting people go past me while I engaged in a silent, yet powerful mental battle with myself.

I so wanted to break this fear and go down the goddamn slide. It was only a waterslide after all – it was meant to be fun. There were small kids going down, beaming with joy, so I kept telling myself that it could not be that bad. It was one of those slides that looked like a huge skateboarding ramp. You sat in an inflatable ring and you would go rushing down, then you would be shot up the opposite side, before shimmying across the dips and coming to a halt.

On one side of my mental boxing ring was the brave coach Noor, coming out with guns blazing, ready to fight: 'Come on, Noor, you can do this. Show the kids you can beat your fear.'

On the other side was the inner child Noor, who had been traumatized by scary rides for as long as she could remember: 'No, Noor, you are mad. This is high and it's fast, and you might die. Just go back down the stairs, grab your cocktail and get back to being sensible.'

'You wrote a book called *Just F*cking Do It*, so practise what you preach,' coach Noor urged me.

This boxing-ring match of back and forth lasted a few more minutes, before I decided to bloody go down the slide. I saw the next kid excitedly let go of the metal bar and whoosh down into oblivion, and that was it. I said, 'Five, four, three, two, one, there is no going back – I'm going to do it!'

I grabbed the inflatable blue ring and sat my bottom down, as the lifeguard smiled and said, 'Yallah! You will have fun.' And before I had any more chances for the shitty committee to talk me out of it again, I felt him gently push my ring and I began my downward descent in what seemed like a flash. They probably heard me in neighbouring continents, the way I screamed, but I did it! And you know what: it was actually kinda fun. 'I might end up being a thrill-seeker after all,' I told myself. The kids were so proud of me and, more importantly, I was proud of myself.

I share this story because there are a few important waterslide-related lessons for you to take on board. First, no amount of wishing or hoping would have got me down that slide, so that I could have won Brave Mum of the Year award. Instead I needed to place my bum down on the blue ring, hold on to my bikini and take a literal plunge into the pool of water below.

One of the most misconstrued pieces of manifesting advice is that if we know what we want and stay positive, somehow good things will magically happen. So let me be frank here. This is absolutely possible. Yes, in the field of miracles, miracles can happen without action. But the field I want you to play in is the field of creation, and when we create *with* the universe, we must take action. Manifesting requires action, as we are activating the law of attraction. You see, the phrase 'law of attraction' ends in the word 'action' – and we do need to move our butts in the physical world.

Back to the good old video-game analogy for a moment. If you stare at the screen and don't pick up the console, you are not going to win the game. You've got to take the steps to meet the universe halfway, when it comes to manifesting what you desire. Yes, it can be as scary as looking down a huge waterslide, but fear can simply be broken down to being excited without the breath – so don't forget to breathe! It's also really important to stay focused on the rewards that you will reap if you take the action, however uncomfortable it may feel.

Coaching task: write it down

Think about something you desire and spend a few minutes writing down everything you can do in the physical world to make it happen – all the strategies, tactics and steps that you can start taking now in order to move forward.

The right *action*

Even though we need to take action if we want to see our dreams come to fruition quickly and easily, we need to take the *right* action. I could have jumped from the top of the waterslide down to the bottom without even sitting on an inflatable ring, and while I would have made it down to the bottom, I might have broken my neck. That's why the right action is needed.

I call this interchangeably the 'right action', 'inspired action' or 'heart hustle'. Inspired action does what it says on the tin: it stems from a bolt of inspiration, an idea, a zing in your body that makes you want to act. It may feel like a logical move, but I truly believe it comes from a gut feeling driven by your heart's desire.

Imagine trying to go up the stairs of a moving escalator while the escalator is actually moving downwards. Every step you take feels like three as you fight against the natural momentum and flow of the escalator moving in the opposite direction. You will literally feel the resistance as you go against the escalator's natural direction. When it comes to taking action, we need to move *with* the flow of energy and not against it. Yes, you will eventually make it to the top of the escalator even if it's working against you, but you'll most probably trip up, it will definitely take you longer and you'll need to fight against the people coming down past you. This is the difference between action and the *right* action – a feeling of resistance or of flow. When you take enough of the 'wrong' action, which feels resistant, you end up getting frustrated and burnt out.

The main difference between action and the right action is the guiding force behind that action. One of the things that completely changed my life was understanding that, as humans, we are armed with two very special superpowers: the first is our imagination, and the second is intuition; and, contrary to popular belief, Google does not have all the answers, but you do.

Coaching note: follow your instinct

Take a moment to think about times in your life when you felt a gut instinct to do something, and you did it and it paid off. This is the kind of guided action you need to get great at taking. Now think of a time when you did not follow that gut instinct and you regretted it. Becoming aware of these different responses will begin to strengthen your faith in trusting yourself and the internal guidance that you are given.

Divine knowingness

It's not the first time in this book that I've talked about the fact that we are energetic beings made up of several layers of energy. Your physical human self is the part that vibrates at a lower speed. This is why we can see it with the human eye. Let's call this your 'human self'. There's also another layer to you: the spiritual self where your soul resides. I like to see our soul as the heart of the spiritual self, holding the wisdom of many lives. Our spiritual self is part of the huge ocean of consciousness and intelligence, and is therefore way smarter than the intelligence centre of the human mind – our brain. Our brains rely on data perceived by the senses, but there's some data that simply doesn't make it to the logical brain and so we feel it in our bodies, hence the words 'gut feeling'. This is our intuition in action, and I see it as a divine knowingness.

That's because, for me, sometimes it's more than a gut feeling; it's a full-body visceral response where every hair on my body stands up and my skin suddenly looks oh-so-goosey. This is your spiritual self communicating with your physical self, giving you guidance.

Intuition is our internal intelligence system that is hooked up to the motherboard of all intelligence – the universe. The word 'intuition', when broken into parts, becomes 'in-tuition', which I like to see as receiving guidance/tuition from within. Have you ever heard the saying 'They've got insider information'? That's how I like to see intuition. It's the powerful purveyor of insider information. It often defies logic, is delicately nagging and persistent and is never wrong. This insider information is ready to connect to us and guide us to take the right action towards our desires, but most of us can't feel or don't trust it, because we don't have a strong connection to it.

Have you ever desperately wanted to get reception on your phone and found yourself frantically running around the whole house to find that one spot that connects? The great thing about intuition is that we are always connected, but for most of us the connection is weak, and we need to find that sweet spot in our lives where we can reconnect to the motherboard, so that we can be guided effortlessly in the direction of our dreams.

When I say 'effortlessly' I don't mean that it will be easy. I don't mean there won't be challenges or obstacles, or things that will test who you are as a person, on your journey to pursuing your most successful life. But this will be the simplest route to get to where you can harness the natural flow of energy and take steps along that yellow brick road towards your very own Oz. The action may force you to face fears, push you outside your comfort zone and ask that you step the heck up, but you will not be able to shake the feeling that it's right for you. After all, Dorothy had to go through quite a few challenges, even though she was on the right road. That's why it's very important that you become self-aware about the feelings in your body, are honest about what it is you want and have that fixed goal in your mind.

Part of the journey to becoming successful is finding that strong connection back to yourself, because when you do, all the ideas, inspiration and guidance you need in order to create your best life and become wildly successful in all aspects will be delivered to you like a beautiful gift, wrapped in gorgeous paper and tied with a bow. I call these 'divine downloads'. It is like infinite intelligence literally placing

The Method

the exact things you need into your mind for you to download and execute. Thomas Edison, who invented the light bulb, used to say that ideas came out of space. He said that while sometimes the ideas seemed astonishing or impossible, they were meant for him. And let's be honest, he made a massive difference to how humans live today, so you gotta trust a guy who didn't give up on his inspiration.

Many of us spend our lives searching for answers outside ourselves, totally negating the fact that we are actually pretty f*cking smart when we tap and tune into our most powerful source of information and inspiration. We just need to have faith. A full and powerful vision in our imagination can always manifest in concrete form as long as we have faith. Faith strengthens the imagination and establishes the will to take action. The world is filled to the brim with people who have worked hard, but don't have much to show for it. This goes back to what I talked about earlier in the book: hard work does not equate with success; there's something bigger. It's trusting those divine downloads and having a belief in your ability to execute those ideas – which means taking the right action. The most successful people have created their success not through the manual labour of their hands, but by using their hands to execute all the incredible ideas that popped into their mind, seemingly out of space.

Once you have become clear in your vision and have activated it in the quantum field, you will start to be guided to take the right action. Trust this information, however it comes. The writer Neville Goddard suggested that once we have activated what we want in the universal field, a bridge of incidents will start to form that will lead us where we want to go, just like the yellow brick road that led Dorothy. When you begin to operate with the belief that what you want is on its way, it's like the bricks of that yellow brick road begin to fall automatically into place. What may appear to be coincidences are actually not, but represent a pattern unfolding that started with you planting your desire in the quantum field.

I want you to note that even though intuition means to be taught from within, sometimes the guidance can also come from outside you, when intelligence beyond you gives you a helping hand – such as repeating numbers showing up, or a specific animal appearing randomly. I always like to look up the meanings of this stuff, because I simply don't believe in coincidences any more, especially if I get a strong 'feeling' that something is there for me to make sense of it.

Learning to trust your gut feeling means learning to trust yourself. This is something we need to master as adults, because from a young age, as humans, we are taught to trust the opinions of others, and so we become less and less in tune with what *we* want and how we feel. We rely so heavily on the opinions of others that we forgo our own ideas and intelligence. This is a bad idea! Most people will apply logic to creating success, but in reality, in order to create success – success that is wilder than your dreams – we need to do plenty of very illogical things. That is why this journey forces you to confront all your demons along the way, because when you start to dive into the realm of the unknown, your brain will want to shut that shit down quicker than you can say 'Christopher Robin'. That's why going for your big dreams is not for the faint-hearted. You need to learn to trust in the unknown, follow a part of you that you probably left behind for most of your life and take inspired action, without having the safety net of predictable results.

Intentional action towards your dreams is a necessary requirement for manifesting. As I have said, miracles can happen, but when you are consciously working towards something, you better believe that sitting on your backside eating Oreos while catching up on *Friends* isn't going to cut it! The way we can take action is by breaking down our vision into milestones and goals. We then work towards those goals with joy and consistency.

We need to create a habit of making our dreams matter and taking consistent action towards them. Sometimes the action isn't easy and forces us to make difficult choices, try new things and step well and truly out of our comfort zone. It's like wearing a new pair of shoes that look amazing, but hurt like hell and give you blisters. You don't give up on those beautiful shoes, you wear them until they become comfortable. Every action stacks upon another action, and you get to witness the impact of the compound effect. Every time we take a step in the direction of our dreams, we become a little more resilient. This resilience grows and, as a result, we grow to be a better energetic match for the bigger things in our lives.

And with each milestone you get to, as you take action, don't forget to celebrate. It's easy for us humans to continue wanting more and more and more – and there's nothing wrong with that, because we are growing and therefore our desires evolve too. However, it's important to take stock of the journey and celebrate along the way, as this gives our lives the meaning and fulfilment that we talked about earlier in this part of the book.

When life can be a continuous sequence of 'Fuck, yes!' moments, that's how we create a 'Fuck, yes!' life. We need to learn to stop and pop that champers and take stock of our sparkly stars, and of the points we gained by killing the baddies. And, most importantly, it's all about having a meaning in life that matters to us.

Let's do a quick summary of what's been covered so far in this part of the book. Get super-clear on a vision that matters, fuelled by your desire and your values. Choose to master your identity, so that your beliefs and thoughts are in alignment and are supporting the cresting of your vision. And, lastly, take inspired and intelligence-led action towards that which you wish to manifest.

Coaching note: a leading question

Ask yourself this one important question: if there was no fear, and only faith, what action would I be taking? This question will help you lead your actions with Big D*ck Energy, which takes us nicely into our next conversation about intention.

Big D*ck Energy

Once your *vision* is nailed, your *identity* is aligned and your *action* plan is in motion, what can you do to make sure that action plan is infused with all the good stuff, so that it is actually actioned, rather than simply looking nice on a piece of paper for the rest of its existence? Well, I once read a study about the sheer power of focused energy, which showed that if you put one focused laser beam against a surface and just left it there, pointing all its energy on one spot, over time the laser beam would pierce a hole. The compound effect of that energy on one surface was enough to make a strong impact on it and eventually burn through it. But how does this have anything to do with you manifesting your dreams?

The study showed how if scientists put something in front of that laser beam, which consequently split the beam into several points, the strength of each of the multiple laser beams was less focused. The result was that each of the individual laser beams did not create energy strong enough to pierce the surface and make a hole. It was the same *overall* amount of energy, but not all in one *focused* area.

This got me thinking deeply about how, as humans, the importance of our focus and attention on a task is imperative. I always say that where attention goes, energy flows and manifestation grows. So if we take focused action in the direction of our biggest dream, the compound effect of that focus and attention will hugely impact upon the result.

Every single successful person I have ever had the pleasure of coming across has one thing in common: their commitment to their vision for life, and the choice to direct their focused energy towards what they want to achieve, with assured self-confidence that it's non-negotiable to achieve this. As I wrote this down, the words that came to my mind were 'Big D*ck Energy'. What do I mean by this? Well, the dictionary tells me it's slightly vulgar slang for the 'attractive aura exuded by a person who has understated, but unshakeable self-confidence' – and actually has zero to do with having a penis. So, to the ladies reading this, we can all exude BDE. Consider the following:

- It's really easy to sit down and make a vision board.
- It's easy to talk about what your dreams are.

- It's easy to spend time visualizing them.
- However, it's not so easy to commit every single day to making it actually happen.

That's why successful people are intentional about how they do everything in life, and they show up with the energy of *confidence without cockiness* – also known as Big D*ck Energy.

An intention is how you *intend* to do something – it's the energy that you put behind a goal. Intentions pierce holes through glass ceilings and help you break through to the next level. Your goal might be to lose weight, but the intention behind it could be 'with focus and commitment'. If you don't have a strong intention that you will take at each step, then you will set goals, but will have no intention of actually making them happen. We can all create a pretty vision board, but it's what we intend to do in order to make it happen that will subsequently result in success or not.

How do you intend to start your day, your week, your month, your year? Start each day with a positive intention about how you wish that day to be. Your intention is the energy you bring to everything that you do. Successful people come with the right intention – I guess you could say it's similar to attitude, but I see an attitude as being a bit broader, and intention as something more laser-focused.

Caspar, my son, was turning one and we had a photoshoot planned, so we wanted to give his hair a little trim. It was his first haircut at a hairdresser's, and since my girls never had haircuts till way later on, this was a whole new experience for us! The hairdresser said she would cut his hair if Caspar could stay still. Both Richard and I had set the intention that this would be a successful hairdressing trip and that we would walk away with Caspar with a fresh trim.

We sat Caspar down on the chair, and the hairdresser walked over and within moments said, 'I won't be able to do a proper cut for him.'

I found that statement super-strange. 'He only needs a few strands trimmed around his ears and at the back,' I said.

'I won't be able to get it straight, though, as he's a baby,' she replied.

'No worries, just do the best you can,' I said as I looked at Richard, wondering if he could feel the negativity seeping out of her pores too.

So the hairdresser starts cutting and Caspar inquisitively turns his head to look. Richard and I tried to keep him entertained while holding his head, and she repeated once again that it wasn't going to be easy and she didn't want to cut him – or cut herself.

We walked out with a haircut, and Caspar looked as cute as a button. As we left, I looked at Richard and said, 'Wow, that lady went into that haircut with absolutely no intention of getting it done as best she could.' She went in with a defeatist attitude, and seemingly had zero desire to do her best job.

From the customer-service standpoint, it was pretty shocking; but on a personal level, I felt like I wanted to give her a hug, tell her to have more confidence in herself and to at least put us at ease by trusting her own abilities. Of course I didn't say that, because she is not my client and shoving my opinions on people when they have not requested them is not something that I see as good social etiquette. But it really got me thinking about the power of intention when it comes to executing anything.

I learned from the lovely Jim Rohn that we should do everything with the best of intentions. Do everything you do with passion, confidence and excitement; start with the intention to do your best work and give it your best go. When I sat down to write my second book, *You Only Live Once*, every time I sat down I set the intention that this book would be a *Sunday Times* bestseller. I infused that intention on every page. And, well, it did become one.

When I started my first business, my intention was to 'make it a little side-hustle'. That intention was the energy guiding everything I did. It was the underlying current that my desire to create freedom sat upon. I played small because I was scared to go all in. I was too scared to say, 'I'm going to make this f*cking work!'

When I began my coaching business I had done a fair bit of

personal development by that point and my intention was very different. I intended to take this business so seriously. I intended to show up as the CEO from day one. I set up a limited company before I'd even put it out there that I was a coach. The energy I brought to the table was non-f*cking-negotiable. There was no Plan B, there was no 'little business energy'; there was only 'I'm all goddamn in – let's do this and make it my mission.'

Imagine how different that hairdresser would have been, how different the experience would have been for all of us, if she had shown up with that energy and intention. When your intention is fuelled by all the good vibes, you actually begin to generate energy from that joy. When a guy walks into the room with his confidence brimming over the edges because he knows he's got the goods, that energy is felt by all – this is Big D*ck Energy in action. But you don't need to be a guy to have this energy. It's the energy of *I can* and *I will*.

Think about it. Think about tasks you don't really want to do, think about your state of mind. Think about the posture of your body, and how motivated you are to do it. It's been proven that your body's posture affects your mental state, and your mental state affects everything you do. When that hairdresser walked over, her body was slouched, her head was kinda low and her voice was monotone. I don't know what had happened in her life until that day. That morning she may have received terrible news and therefore she was showing a reflection of that, which is why I am actually pretty good at not being judgemental about such things any more. However, for the purpose of this example, let's imagine that was just how she showed up at work, and she felt fine.

Now imagine if she had raised her shoulders, set the intention that she was going to deliver an amazing haircut, took the time to engage with Caspar, make him smile and put him at ease, and even put us at ease as parents – and then smiled and enjoyed her experience. For her own mental health, the experience would have been so different.

Becoming self-aware that you are going to execute things successfully will change everything for you. When you intend to do things in a certain way that gears you to succeed, you generate energy in your body, you increase the motivation in your brain and you enjoy the process of doing what you need to, and the results are something you will be happy with.

Have you ever in your life heard a dentist exclaim to you that he is the luckiest man alive because he put a filling in beautifully? Well, I have! Before he began drilling and filling my pesky tooth, he said with confidence, 'This will be the best filling you have ever had.' The pride in his work and his love for his job shone through, and I felt so honoured to have been in his dentist's chair while he did his life's work on me. I wanted to smile, but I couldn't feel half my face as he gave me extra anaesthetic so that I could 'enjoy' the experience! Once he was done, he explained in this amazingly thick Italian accent, 'That is the most beautiful filling. I am so happy. I am the luckiest man alive. This will fix everything!'

To be on the receiving end of that was wonderful, but for him showing up at work every day was not a burden, but a joy. When you manifest like this, your energy changes and you become a magnet for *more* – more of everything that you desire. The desire is what you want, and your intention is how you intend to go about making that desire a reality.

Coaching task: post your intention

Think about the tasks you need to do this month. Now think about the intention with which you will show up in order to do those things. For example, 'I am focused/grounded/enthusiastic/determined/energized.' Write down three words that will help you commit and embody that intention. I sometimes like to write them on a Post-it Note and stick it on my laptop, so that I remember it daily.

Knowledge isn't power

Before we dive into the final part of the book, I want to wrap up this part and the conversation around *Action* by explaining something really powerful that helped me actually *move* towards what I wanted. This one simple thing is that knowledge isn't power. There are some really smart people who have filled their brains with copious amounts of information about everything they could possibly know. What is truly powerful is taking that knowledge and applying it. Application of knowledge and *relentless action* are where the power truly lies.

Many incredibly smart people get stuck in the land of learning and never make it onto the path of progression because they want to keep consuming more and more information, as though it's a safety net. Don't be one of those people! Take what I've taught you in this book and apply it. Or, if you wish to work further to really master what I teach, come and join me in one of my coaching experiences. You can check them out here: www.thisisyourdream. com / workwithme.

Success is not about being the smartest person in the room, but the most determined, which is why sometimes we won't have the right knowledge, but finding people who do have that knowledge is something every successful person I have met is very good at. I've come to see that the quality of your life will be determined by the quality of the questions that you are willing to ask. I always ask my business clients at the end of our monthly call, 'What questions do you need answering, so that you can move towards what you desire?' If *you* don't know the answers, I can assure you there is someone who does. Find that someone. Find the person who has got where you want to be and ask them for their help, their mentorship or their guidance.

I've got to where I am today, with four kids, by recognizing that there are people with greater knowledge and skills than I have and, if I learn from them, I'm going to compress the time it would have taken to get there myself. Sometimes the action we need to take is finding the people who can help us move forward.

This is a fundamental trait of successful people – they are not scared to ask for directions. Why try to find the way alone, at the risk of getting lost for hours, when you can be given clear instructions and a roadmap? It doesn't make you less of a person to ask for help; in fact I think it makes you smart and resourceful.

For years I wanted to learn how to invest in the stock market, but it terrified me. I read countless books on investing, but it wasn't until I invested in a course with someone that I resonated with, who broke it down for me in simple steps, that I finally had the confidence to go and invest myself. I'm now building my long-term wealth on the stock markets. Having support from someone who's made mistakes and who can help you is invaluable. That's why investing in yourself is one of the best things any of us can do, if we have the desire to move quickly towards our future life.

Coaching note: question yourself

Every month as you plan how to move forward, ask yourself, 'What questions do I need answering? What support do I need?' Then finding the answers to the questions, and the support you need, is actually super-simple.

PART THREE

The Mastery

12.

Supercharging your success

Success is not about being the best. It's about always getting better and growing. That's why this part of the book is about mastering yourself. Now that you have defined what success means to you, and you are armed with the steps for transforming your life, it's time to figure out what could come in between you and your dreams – and how to overcome that. At some level we all have an internal glass ceiling created by our beliefs, and those ceilings are what block us from reaching the next level of the video game of our lives.

In order to move forward and smash through these ceilings, we need to first address the elephant in the room. Okay, not one elephant, but five elephants! These elephants represent each of the different success blockers that I've seen coming between humans and their big dreams. Each success blocker is the result of the subconscious scripts we have created that are no longer serving us and are keeping us hostage to our current life.

So let me introduce these pesky little blockers: fear, money stories, limiting beliefs, negative self-image and misaligned energy. I'll be sharing the cause of each of these blockers, the consequences they have on creating our best life and, finally, how to use Subconscious Rescripting® so that you rewrite the stories that your unconscious mind is telling you and manifest your dreams with ease. Let me make this clear from the get-go: at some level we have *all* of these blocking us. They all kinda bleed into one another and are not entirely separate, but if we can try to compartmentalize them, then we can begin to start smashing through the blocks bit by bit.

One thing to note: successful people aren't successful because they are lucky or haven't got any resistance or blockers. But through personal mastery, they get better and better at identifying these success blockers and then releasing their stronghold and smashing through that next glass ceiling. If you haven't already gathered this from the first two parts of my book, your energy is your life, and mastery of your energetic vibration is the key to creating and manifesting the life you desire. So mastery of our success blockers essentially means mastery of our mind, our vibration, and constant conscious curating of our energy. When you understand why these cause you to feel the way you do and how to change them, you start operating from a place of personal power.

'Personal power' refers to the power you have within yourself, independent of external circumstances or unconscious programming. Personal power allows you to create your own opportunities, take risks and navigate challenges with confidence. When we have personal power, we can become aware of our blocks and call them out for what they are: useless!

One vital thing to remember is that our subconscious mind is working tirelessly to keep us safe and survive. It doesn't stop us because it wants us to fail; it stops us because it thinks it's helping. Because it stored all our past experiences as references to anything that can potentially cause us stress, it's ready and waiting to put up a big metaphorical 'Stop' sign as we move forward out of our oh-so-comfy zone. This Stop sign represents the resistance/blocks that we feel.

As we go into this part of the book, what you will start to understand more deeply is that when the subconscious mind puts up that Stop sign, it causes our sympathetic nervous system to activate, which then causes us to feel stress, which shows up in varying ways. My perspective is that this stress is a glitch or dysfunction, and it's the biggest reason why most people don't move forward. And so, as you will come to see, part of overcoming those blocks is by understanding how to regulate your nervous system.

When we can regulate our nervous systems, we become masters of our own energy. Then, once it is regulated, we can begin to rewrite and activate a new story, thus producing new results in our lives. So through understanding what our bodies are trying to tell us at any given moment and having the ability to consciously calibrate this, we take back our personal power and can rewrite the story of our subconscious mind. This truly is the most powerful work I've ever done, and it continues to make a hugely positive impact on my clients.

I have worked with thousands of incredible and capable people, and when I ask them what's stopping them from going for their dream, it's unbelievable how many say, 'I'm scared.' In fact I did a survey and a staggering 66 per cent said that fear was the thing blocking them. That's why I am going to cover fear first, because this is always the head honcho of success blockers and spills over into everything. Once you understand fear in a different way, you will be able to finally take control of it, like you haven't been able to before.

13

Success Blocker #1: Fear

Never have I seen a more accurate acronym than FEAR (*False Evidence Appearing Real*) to describe what most humans go through as they try to start a new business or endeavour in their lives. You will see very shortly why this acronym is so fitting. Fear shows up in absolutely every single person I've ever helped, in some shape or form, and when you start to see how it's actually false evidence appearing real, your mind will be blown.

As I shared earlier, our powerful mind is processing data each and every millisecond. When the mind detects a *potential* threat, it sends signals to the amygdala, a small almond-shaped structure in the brain that plays a key role in processing emotions pretty darn quickly. The words 'potential threat' are very important here.

The amygdala subsequently activates the sympathetic nervous system, which prepares the body to respond to the perceived danger by releasing stress hormones such as adrenaline and cortisol. This triggers the well-known fight-or-flight response, causing an increase in heart rate, blood pressure and breathing rate among other physiological changes, such as increased strength, in case you need to run from the bogeyman or drop-kick a mugger. This fight-or-flight response is ingrained in every single animal and human, but there is a fundamental difference between us and the other animals in how this primitive response has been installed and, due to this fundamental difference, our fight-or-flight response is prone to dysfunction.

This is because, as humans, we have a conscious and a subconscious mind; we essentially have two components that are responsible for different things. Our conscious mind has evolved greatly and has surpassed that of other animals *hugely* – it has received the memo that it's the twentieth century and we are not primitive creatures living in the wild. We know that our conscious mind has evolved compared to that of other mammals because humans – in contrast to lions, say – can put men on the moon, cook a steak on a barbecue and film a TikTok video.

However, the subconscious mind (which is primitive in nature) has not evolved anywhere near as much, and it still reacts as though we are living in the wild and is constantly on alert for potential dangers. This causes a conflict in communication between the conscious and subconscious minds, a dysfunction that can lead to anxiety and other negative effects on our physical and mental health.

This is why we can logically say things like 'It's only a waterslide', as in my story earlier, yet still feel a disproportionate and somewhat irrational fear. The conscious mind may be speaking the King's English in the clearest of voices, but the subconscious hears 'Blah-blah, blah-blah, blah-blah.'

Another extraordinary thing about our subconscious mind is that it cannot tell the difference between reality and imagination. Let me prove this to you: close your eyes and imagine yourself, in as much detail as possible, going to your kitchen, grabbing a lemon, smelling it, cutting it and then sucking on it. Do that now and bring in as much sensory data as you can. What people experience is quite remarkable: lips pucker, mouths salivate and there is a physical reaction to an imaginary lemon. Your mind sends signals to your body, even in the absence of a real lemon.

Now I'm truly sorry to do this to you, but it's important that you grasp the power of your mind. Imagine something bad happening to someone you love. For me, in just a nanosecond of thinking something bad is happening to my kids, I can feel a tsunami of fear rise in my body. I can almost feel myself getting nauseous. Even when we just think about something going wrong, our minds will begin to send the signals to our physical bodies quicker than you can say 'Christopher goddamn Robin'.

Lastly, I want you to think about something that happened in the past that still bothers you today – an event that had a high emotional charge. Bring up the feelings for just a few seconds . . . and stop. Our unconscious minds cannot discern between past, present and future and if your mind hasn't processed emotion properly from the past, then it believes it's still happening now. It's like when you play with sand at the beach and you try to sieve the sand but, because it's wet, it gets stuck together in globs. Those old, unprocessed experiences are like globs and, unlike any other species, as humans we can get stuck in the trauma of the past that no longer exists, become anxious about a future that is worrisome but also doesn't exist, and this causes us to be stuck in a present that feels less than peaceful.

Many people *feel* the fear of a threat that isn't actually there. Why? This false evidence of danger (in the absence of something physically threatening) activates the fight-or-flight response, but since going for your dream doesn't require you to flee from anything or bite a predator in anger, the mind gets caught in limbo and you feel 'stuck'. This is a comment I heard a lot from people who want to move forward towards creating their best life.

This has highly damaging consequences. When we begin to have a visceral fear-based reaction to things that aren't actually threats, what happens to some people is that they fear these symptoms of the heart racing, sweaty palms, energy coursing through their body (the physical symptoms of fear), and this fear of the defence mechanism creates what we know as anxiety.

As you can see, the mind is powerful, but unless we get our conscious and subconscious minds communicating effectively and processing old emotions, we get stuck. When it comes to being scared, it's vital that we learn to discern the difference between reality and imagination, and that we override the mind's ability to create fear that isn't real.

Identifying the fear

My job is first to figure out what my client's mind is processing as fear, so that I can use Subconscious Rescripting® to get them not only to regulate their nervous system, but also to activate a new set of belief systems. This is where things get interesting and there is a plot twist.

Could it be fear that going for their dreams may result in losing their limbs? Are there potential dangers or four-eyed monsters waiting to eat them, finger by finger? Could it be that they will be faced with terrorists strapped to bombs? Or, even worse, death? After all, they are willing to stay stuck, overwhelmed and living a life that drains them, rather than going for their dream, due to this fear . . . So there must be something really f*cking scary.

'I'm scared I *might* fail,' they say.

'I'm scared people *might* judge me,' they gasp.

'What if I cannot make it a success and I *might* have to go back to what I was doing before?' they exclaim.

Wait, there are no lions or tigers or bears! There's no four-eyed Gruffalo with teeth the size of Everest, waiting to maul you! I've never heard anyone answer to me that they are scared of dying or becoming chronically ill from going for their dreams, but they are terrified of failing or being judged.

It's like sitting down to watch the world's most non-scary horror movie: *The Wrath of the Might*. You have popcorn in your hands, your head already tucked into your shirt in anticipation, as three girls go wandering into a dark wood at night. The music in the background is adding to the fear as you wait with bated breath, knowing that something bad is about to happen. Will there be an axe-murderer, or the *Scream* mask-guy, or Chucky? Your heart is racing and you begin to bite the nails on your sweaty palm as you shout in your head, 'Do not go further into the woods!' – and then the movie just finishes.

All that fear, that build-up, that suspense of thinking about everything, little things that might go wrong – and then nothing! The mind is great at building up all the suspense, for no actual horror. The minds of my incredible clients have built up these huge pictures of fear, and illustrious stories of their own demise, which they begin to experience as physical signs of anxiety and fear, even where there is none.

For most people, going for your dream is *not* going to place you in a dangerous or unsafe situation. *Read that again.* It may put you in an *uncomfortable* situation that pushes how you feel emotionally, but 99 per cent of the time you are not in an unsafe position that requires fear. I'm saying '99 per cent' because I don't know what your dream is. If your dream is flying out of a plane, then I'd like to leave 1 per cent leeway because, frankly, that may be unsafe!

So what can you do to stop this fear glitch from happening? How do you stop your mind processing the information incorrectly and causing you to go into a state of fear? Well, this is the work I do on my courses, programmes and in private coaching. By communicating to the mind in the right way, we can effectively give the memo that there's not a real fear out there. Usually fear is coming up because of a past experience that wasn't processed properly, so my job is to help the mind process it effectively so that the 'glob' goes through the sieve. Past experiences that caused us distress are sometimes left open, like tabs on the computer screen of our mind, and will remain open until we close them down – which is the work that I do with my clients. Then we teach the mind new sets of stories and scripts that are conducive to success.

There are things that you can start doing yourself. First, it's essential that you become hyper-vigilant over what you worry about, and over the thoughts you allow to occupy your headspace. If you keep worrying about the same stuff going wrong, your body will have a physical reaction, thus repeating the thoughts and locking you into a state of worry and anxiety over something that is not real any more. You need to stop that negative feedback circuit by telling yourself there's nothing to be scared of. Breathe deeply and slowly, as this will switch on your parasympathetic nervous system, which is like pushing down the brake in a car. It starts to slow down the fight-or-flight or freeze response.

You need to embrace the discomfort of stepping into something new, of taking yourself out of your oh-so-comfy zone, or you will struggle to reach the next levels of the video game and transcend to new levels of being. Being uncomfortable is not the same as being in danger, and as soon as you let your mind know that, things will change.

Why, as humans, do we see 'failure' or judgement by others as being as scary as being mauled by a wild animal? The simple answer is that humans were designed to live in tribes, because this was vital for survival. Back in the days when our crib was more cave than cul-de-sac, we would live in our own tribes, each with their own set of rules. We would stick strongly to those rules because being shunned by the tribe meant banishment, starvation and eventually death.

Our primitive mind therefore seeks to belong, for the primary reasons of safety and survival. We are also designed to be with others because, as humans, we need connection. This is why it's no surprise that loneliness is the biggest precursor to depression and suicide. We don't want to be lonely, we don't want to starve or be excluded from the tribe and we certainly don't want death, so at an unconscious level we always want to do whatever the tribe wants, even if there are no more caves and it's the twenty-first century. As I said before, the subconscious mind never got the memo.

In this modern day, our tribe is our family and our close social network. While they may not banish you from the village if you break the unspoken rules they have set, you may face a fate far worse than being stoned to death: *judgement*. Since your primitive mind hasn't evolved that much since caveman days and still operates at the same level as a zebra, it has a hard time understanding that most things are not actually a threat, and so even judgement by those closest to you can feel like a dagger to the heart. Even worse, simply the thought of judgement by others has the power to do the same thing.

So we do things in life even if they don't feel right for us because we are driven by the invisible, yet palpable expectations of our tribes and by the unconscious need to *belong*, even if it doesn't serve us. And fear of breaking the rules keeps us stuck. That's why it's so hard to break the mould of a subconscious belief, as it feels unsafe to our mind.

Breaking the mould

Many people find it hard to become the first entrepreneur in a family who have had generations of doctors. It may feel difficult to say, 'I want to marry someone of a different religion or colour' (or replace this with other things that you feel go against the unspoken rules of your tribe). Many people keep themselves small and are not honest about what they want, because of the fear of disappointing others and, consequently, of being judged. Being judged is worse than most other fates, because then we feel that we aren't liked, don't belong and will be rejected by those we love.

But it's time to break free from this, because living a life confined to a small box of possibilities is far worse than being banished. At least if you are banished you can do what you want! So how can we overcome these unspoken rules and pave the way for forming life on our own terms?

First, find the courage to have honest conversations with other people, without attack or defence. Love and compassion are the best ways of starting to break through the unspoken rules of our tribes. If people don't want to accept you for who you are, then you need to ask yourself how willing you are to keep yourself small in order to keep them happy, as you only live this one life on Earth. Are you willing to sacrifice your own happiness to feel like you belong? Or are you brave enough to find a new tribe?

It's quite extraordinary how thoughts of an 'honest' conversation with a primary caregiver can put the fear of God into someone. However, from working with my clients, I've seen the unfolding of the most beautiful sequence of events and deeper bonds when people let down their guards, have difficult conversations and start to break down the barriers of the unspoken rules that have been holding them hostage for years. Taking the time to understand your parents' conditioning will be incredibly valuable, as it will give you insights into why they are as they are, with a level of empathy that shows you that it's not their fault.

We also need to contend with our 'extended tribes'. The dawn of social media has been incredible for the rise of opportunities and business-building, but the dark side is that we no longer feel judgement just from our immediate tribe; we now feel the wrath of judgement from our 'extended tribes' on social media, which encompass complete strangers 3,000 miles away across the globe.

One of the shadow sides of going out and building my business in the public arena has been attracting people who like to be mean, for no apparent reason other than to be mean. I have to admit that at the start it was hard. People were writing comments about how annoying I sounded on my audio book, calling me a scammer, making comments about how I created my videos or my book, and writing personal digs that hit me in the jugular. All I wanted to do was help people, so why were they attacking me?

As the years went by, I started to realize something: it wasn't about *me*. It was always about them. I've never gone out of my way in life to be nasty to someone for no reason. I've never made personal digs about someone else on a public platform. The truth is that as you create a life that's better than your dreams, other people (humanoids) start to see that and it begins to hold a mirror up to their own lives. Once you start shining your own bright light, it will do one of two things. Either it will light up and inspire other people to create their own dream life, or it will expose people's flaws and show them where they wish their life could be, but they will feel so uncomfortable at being exposed that they will project their discomfort back to you.

I've worked on my subconscious mind so much that when these things happen now, instead of my nervous system going into overdrive and causing me anxiety, my mind understands that it's not a threat to my safety and survival. I'm no longer a twelve-year-old with no help or support to fight the bullies. I no longer need the approval of strangers on the internet, instead I focus on those I can help. My life is not in danger, I won't get thrown out of the tribe and these people are here to make me *stronger*, so that I can be resilient enough to make a bigger impact. Such people will judge you if you don't win, and they will judge you if you do. You will never please them all, so why expend beautiful energy doing so.

I've come to learn that the courage to be successful also includes the courage to be disliked. This is your life – your one chance of creating a masterpiece – and as long as you are doing it with grace and integrity, let them judge and hate you; just delete and block them. So that's what I do now. Adios! Au revoir! Ciao!

When you are disliked by someone, it's proof that you are exercising your freedom and living in alignment with what you want, and it's a great sign that you are doing what you desire. You can't change people, but you can change how you respond to them. Choose to send love to the person who throws you shade, knowing that in order for that person to feel so strongly about you, you must have triggered something in them. They have chosen to take that discomfort and throw it right back at you, but you can choose to put up your umbrella of love and protect yourself. The more you send someone love, the less those words will affect you.

Coaching note: find self-awareness

If you get triggered by someone, then I'd like to offer you a tool. See it as something being activated in you and use that moment as a point of self-awareness. What did they say? How is it making me feel? What is it giving me? What action must I take? Is it happening because of something that is occurring now or because of something in my past that needs to be healed and dealt with?

The fear of failure

It's reported that Thomas Edison took almost 10,000 attempts to invent the light bulb. Ten freaking thousand! And yet most people give up after one go and throw in the dream and the crazy ideas. Imagine if Edison had given up on the 100th go.

J. K. Rowling got rejected twelve times before anyone considered

Harry Potter to be a viable concept. I got rejected multiple times when trying to get a book deal. If it was so easy to go for these big-ass dreams, then everyone would be living their best lives. It takes some grit in the game, and some mental discipline to tell yourself that what is happening in the 3D world right now is not a reflection of what is possible. It's simply a reflection of what's happening *now* – not for ever. Being able to experience the now and still hold a strong vision for the future is the game we must play if we want to create the amazing stuff of our dreams.

In the field of manifestation where we create extraordinary things, we need to be okay with not knowing the outcome. We need to be okay with throwing the dart at the board and recognizing that we may not get a bullseye the first, the second or even the third time. We cannot be scared of failing, because failing can only exist in a world where you see your first failure as the final answer. You need to have the tenacity and gumption to say, 'Okay, this didn't go the way I wanted the first time, but I'll pivot, I'll tweak and I'll keep going.'

If you have a dream in your heart, as I did about being an author, then you need to trust that dream *more* than you trust your fear; you need to trust that dream *more* than every rejection or physical sign that things aren't going right. I once read that fear is excitement without the breath, so remember to breathe when you are faced with the impending doom of something scary. You need to keep telling yourself, 'The universe doesn't say *no*, but it may say *not yet*.'

Every time you fall or fuck up on the way to your dream, know that it's happening *for* you: for your growth, for your resilience, for the strong person you need to become on the way to getting to the destination you desire. You can't give up or be scared of invisible monsters that don't exist. You need to get good at drinking pints of fear and checking always 'Am I unsafe or am I uncomfortable?' Make a decision based solely on the truth of your answer. And, of course, do not forget to breathe. Breathe deeply and remind yourself *why* you are doing what you are doing, and remember that your dreams are depending on you.

14.

Success Blocker #2: Money stories

When I say the words, 'Money is . . . ', what thoughts and feelings come up for you?

- Money is . . . coins?
- Money is . . . paper?
- Money is . . . good/bad/annoying?
- Money is . . . stressful?
- Money is . . . a taboo subject to talk about, so how dare you bring it up, Noor?

Think about how you feel when someone talks about money. Think about how it would feel to ask someone how much they earn. Think about how you feel about very wealthy people. Think about how you feel about your own financial situation.

Considering these simple, yet powerful statements will provide you with valuable insights into your own relationship with money – one of the most important relationships you will ever have in the duration of your lifetime on this planet. We will call this relationship your 'money story'.

The reason your money story is a blocker for success is because, sadly, for many people it's a dysfunctional and often toxic relationship, rather than a healthy, loving one where there is mutual trust and respect. Some people treat money like it's a one-night stand, spending every penny the minute it comes in, for a quick thrill; others are the over-protective, possessive partner, hoarding money, not letting it go out to have any fun, constantly in fear that it may leave them one day. Some people commit to money in the long term and like to see it grow, while others prefer immediate gratification. But one thing I'm almost certain of is that most people engage unconsciously in this relationship with money. And for the most part, our story about money is driven by a lack of understanding of what money really is, so let's start with that.

Money is the most misunderstood resource on this planet, and what I'm about to share with you might just blow your mind . . . *Money doesn't really exist.*

'Well, of course it does, Noor. What the hell are you talking about, you crazy person? Money is very much something that exists, and I don't have enough of it and I'm stressed. Now we must burn you at the stake!'

You may want to shout at me, but before your mind starts boggling at this sentiment: yes, money does exist in the literal sense, but stick with me while I go into this a little further. The concept of money has become so ingrained in our daily lives that it's hard to imagine a world without it. However, some philosophers and economists argue that money is nothing more than a social construct – a shared belief that certain objects or numbers have a certain value. In this view, money does not have any inherent value of its own.

When you hold a coin or a paper note, you are holding money. So yes, it does physically exist, but when I asked Siri on my iPhone (the purveyor of all information in my world) what a coin was, Siri kindly pulled up this definition: 'A flat disc or piece of metal with an official stamp, used *as* money.' I've italicized the 'as'. That 'as' insinuates that the piece of metal represents something. Rub out the 'official stamp' and the number, and it's no more than a worthless lump of metal. A paper note itself is worthless; it's the printed number on it that makes it worth something, as it represents an amount of 'something'.

When you log into your online banking and see the numbers on the screen, they are simply that: numbers on a screen. Numbers that, within a flash and the click of a button, can jump from one screen to another. Money is simply a representation of something else, usually a physical commodity or a service. This means that the value of money is actually derived from the things it can buy, not from the money itself. The paper, coins and numbers are *representations of value*. They are a symbol of something intangible – a symbol of energy being exchanged.

If you think about the word 'current', it refers to the movement of energy, so it makes sense that a system of money in a particular country is called 'a currency'. Money is a system that humans invented in order to help us exchange our energy output and allow it to flow through society, from one person to another.

But it didn't start like that. Back in the day – way, way back in the day – people would exchange services for services: 'You rub my back, I'll rub yours.' Then, when all the backs had been rubbed and someone didn't necessarily want a back-rub or what the other person was offering, things shifted. A new medium of exchange was introduced: cattle, shells, leather notes and even precious metals were exchanged to represent a value. There wasn't even a standard method of exchange; every country had its own form of currency enabling the flow of energy to circulate, representing a given value.

As time progressed, the gold standard was introduced and money was represented by an equivalent weight in gold. That made complete sense, as there was a measure of value – the weight of gold pertained to an amount of money. Then, as quickly as the gold standard came in, it disappeared, and the current monetary exchange system came into place, which was based on the perceived value of items and services. Now that your history lesson is over, let's have a conversation about why your money story is blocking you.

Each of us has our own money story: our own set of beliefs, attitudes and experiences related to money. It's the narrative that we tell ourselves about our relationship with money, how we view money and how we use it in our lives. A person's money story is mostly shaped by their upbringing, as discussed earlier in the book, their culture and their personal experiences with money. As a child, what you saw (perhaps your parents arguing about money), what you heard (things like 'Money doesn't grow on trees') and what you experienced (not getting what you wanted, because you couldn't afford it) all began to create subconscious scripts about money.

For example, someone who grew up in a family that struggled financially might have a money story that revolves around scarcity and the fear of not having enough. They may view money as something that is hard to come by and feel anxious about spending it. On the other hand, someone who grew up in a wealthy family might have a money story that centres around privilege and entitlement, and may have different beliefs about the value of hard work and financial responsibility.

Sadly, in the world we live in, most of us were exposed as children to narratives about money that were largely negative, which creates a money story that is fuelled by negativity, rather than one fuelled by positive experiences. A negative money story can create a constant feeling of fear and anxiety around finances. You may worry about paying bills, saving for the future or making ends meet, which can lead to stress and a decreased sense of well-being. This in turn creates limiting beliefs about your ability to achieve financial success. You may believe that you're not capable of earning more money or that financial freedom is out of reach, which can hold you back from taking risks and pursuing opportunities.

Coaching note: compare your past with your present

Think about what you saw, heard and experienced as a child when it came to money. Look at your current life and identify any parallels and similarities.

Understanding your own money story

Having a toxic money story will result in you repelling what you desire financially, because your subconscious mind sees money as something bad. If your mind thinks it's bad, then every time you contend with making more money in your life and move yourself out of your comfort zone, your unconscious mind will signal to your sympathetic nervous system that it perceives a threat, producing physical symptoms in your body and thus fear and anxiety. You will then self-sabotage, because it feels safer and more comfortable not to feel the fear, and so you will play small in life when it comes to creating wealth, because unconsciously money has become a threat to you, due to the stories you learned.

When I began the work of understanding my own money story, it changed my whole f*cking life. I do not say this lightly, and I believe this is mandatory work for every single human being on this planet. Understanding your own money story can be a powerful tool in gaining control of your finances and making positive changes. By recognizing the beliefs and attitudes that may be holding you back, you can start using Subconscious Rescripting® to regulate your nervous system around money, to shift your perspective and to adopt new, more empowering beliefs about money.

In addition, it's valuable to recognize the social contracts around money that could potentially be holding you hostage to your current financial situation – the two biggest ones being the value trap and the time trap.

The value trap

Let's talk about the value system for a moment. As humans, *we* decided what energy exchange we charged for everything that was sold, which created the monetary system. And then, as society, we created norms about who was valuable and who wasn't, and we all got sucked into this way of thinking. Essentially a group of people made all this up, and we got born into a system that keeps us fearing money. Furthermore, the value of money can fluctuate greatly, depending on factors such as inflation, economic stability and public perception. What was considered valuable yesterday may not be so valuable today, and what is valuable today may not be so valuable tomorrow. This further reinforces the idea that money is a social construct that is subject to change, based on collective beliefs and values.

When we get a job, our employer has decided the value that we are worth and this is represented in an annual salary. The important point to make about this is that we are capped by how valuable we are deemed to be in our roles, and by the structure of society. For example, bus drivers are deemed to be less valuable by societal norms than psychologists, and this is reflected in the money they are given. This value is usually measured against the skill set. If someone has a skill set that took longer to acquire and is more valuable to customers and consumers, then their salary is higher. That is because not everyone wants, or has the means, to study for seven years to become a clinical psychologist or a doctor, so their wage will reflect that. Their energy output into their role (mental and monetary) determines the energy input (salary) they will receive.

To illustrate this, a bus driver may need a week's training, which is paid for, versus a psychologist who needs seven years' training that *they* have paid for. Can I make it explicitly clear that, as humans, *we are all incredibly valuable* and this has nothing to do with how good a person you are or how hard you work; this is about how the system is rigged against us. Someone can work a physically demanding job for sixty hours a week, but get paid less than someone who works at a desk for ten hours. This brings me to my first lesson: the amount of money you earn is not comparable to how *hard* you work.

The time trap

In traditional job roles we also get restricted by the number of hours we can work. So I go to work for eight hours, the employer decides how valuable I am by giving me a set amount of money per hour, and then I get given that money once I've given my employer the value, which results in the numbers that I see online on my banking screen. Even if the psychologist chose to work every hour of every day of every week of every year, she would be capped, income-wise, at 24/7 over 365 days. And the downside is that she would have to spend all her earnings on every expensive facial treatment there

is out there, to combat the ageing effects of all that sleep depriv-
ation! Joking aside, it's physically impossible. We are bound to the
system, but the amount of time that we can physically work is
limited by how valuable the employer sees us as being, and it feels
really difficult to break out of the mould.

So how do we escape from this system? Well, if the bus driver
decided to go off-piste and create his own bus business, he could
determine his own value. Let's say that one day he gets an amazing
idea. An idea or inspiration represents a greater intelligence coming
through you – the intelligence that wants you to succeed and be
abundant; the intelligence that built you up with a system designed
for you to succeed. It's like your very own universal bank.

The bus driver – let's call him Barry – has an idea that his bus
could have plush velvet seats that are super-comfy for longer jour-
neys. There would be large TVs streaming the latest shows, and a
delicious afternoon tea served to all the customers, thus making the
experience of being on a bus exponentially better. Sounds glorious!
Therefore Barry decides to invest his savings to create this business.
He charges three times more than usual, because he recognizes
how much more valuable his service is, and of course people pay
because they want that better experience over being stuck on a
normal bus.

That idea/thought has now turned into money.

Money is energy. It flows through people, but it *really* comes
from the Source (or God, the universe or whatever other word
you wish to use to describe it). Barry tuned into the motherlode,
accepted his mission and now he has a thriving bus business that
makes him more money in less time, because Barry only works at
weekends and makes more than he did when he was working
forty hours a week. Money is the *result* of the value that we put
out into the world.

If the psychologist realized she didn't want to exchange her
limited time for a capped income, then she could perhaps find a way
to reach and help more people by taking her knowledge and expert-
ise and putting it into a book or a course. Breaking out of the linear

way of thinking as set by societal norms, and recognizing that money isn't just a 'doing' activity, is how we create freedom.

I know that some of you who are reading this book love your jobs, but perhaps not the pay. And that you would love to create more money, but don't necessarily have the desire to set up a 'business'. Well, in that case, you need to be open to creative ways of multiplying your income. Most people are put off any possibilities and tuned into such a negative wavelength that they don't allow ideas to find them.

Ideas create money, and we need to allow those ideas to come through us and then take action on them. We live in a world of duality: where there is hot, there is cold; where there is wet, there is dry; where there is fast, there is slow and where there is a right, there must be a left. So if money is a result in the *outer* world, then there must be something happening in your *inner* world. It all starts with the work that we do within. We get to create and receive as much money as we choose to, when we understand how it works and how to tap into the motherlode.

My first experience of breaking the value and time traps was when I decided to start my first 'proper' business. I'll be frank, I was a bit of a Del Boy in 2013, trying anything to make a quick buck so that I didn't have to go back to my God-awful job after my initial maternity leave. In 2015 I received an email that talked about how to make money by selling products online. It shared mind-blowing and extraordinary success stories. My heart lit up, and yet I was fighting the inner voice that said, 'This isn't possible for you!'

After weeks of researching, I decided to invest in learning how to build an online product business. I spent £2,500 on a course, which was a huge chunk of my savings, and simultaneously felt terrified and excited. The result? I single-handedly created my first brand of beard products. Yes, as in a beard on a man's face! I sold more than £100,000 worth of beard oils, beard balms and beard combs during my second maternity leave, while being a full-time mummy. At the start I worked early mornings and late nights when the kids were asleep to set this up, but once it was all running, I only needed to work for a few hours each week from my laptop and I was making more money than I'd ever done before, without having to answer to any boss. I found a product that was valuable to others, and I sold it online to thousands of people across the world from the comfort of my own home. From then on, something internal had shifted within me about what was truly possible. And I want that for you, too.

When we realize that the monetary system is rigged against us and yet is also an illusion, the way we create more money is by realizing that we don't need to do what is considered 'normal'. We need to break out of average thinking and expand our possibilities beyond the time and value traps, if we want to create real financial freedom.

And we will start with one very important question . . . *How can I be of service to others?*

The world is full of crazy opportunities for people to make more money. I had a chat with our estate agent and she informed me that one of her friends gets paid thousands a month for squishing bananas in between her feet on OnlyFans! I had a fifteen-year-old lad reach out to me on Instagram to ask if I needed help with editing videos. My brother-in-law's sister is a full-time teacher, but sells printables for teachers on Etsy and makes £10k extra a month. There are social-media channels dedicated to showcasing the hundreds of different ways in which you can get paid more for doing a variety of different wild and wonderful, and also very ordinary, things.

So the question given above is one of the most important and lucrative questions you can ask yourself in your lifetime. When you find a solution to a problem, and a way to serve humanity through your unique strengths, gifts and ideas, then you open the floodgates for abundance to come to you and can begin to manifest the most incredible things.

Coaching task: turn your value into income

I want you to imagine that you live in a world before our illusory monetary system was put in place – think about how you would survive. Let's put banana-squishing aside and think about what services you could offer others. How could you help your neighbours and your community? Grab a piece of paper and brainstorm this question as though your life depends on it – pull out *every* single thing you can think of. This is now a list of how you can create more money in your life, if you need it. This is how you can offer value. All of us have the ability to create the life we desire, as long as we are able to see that we are valuable to others and can figure out the best way to turn that value into income.

Right, we have covered some serious ground already in this book and if you've got this far, you are doing amazingly. Your perspectives are beginning to shift, your mind is starting to understand things in a different way and you are now changing the trajectory of your life, my friend. That's bloody exciting!

15.

Success Blocker #3: Limiting beliefs

We have talked a lot in this book already about the power of beliefs, and 'limiting beliefs' kinda do what it says on the tin – they are beliefs that limit you and keep restricting you in some way, rather than propelling you to where you want to go. We have a mental library filled with thousands of beliefs about everything in life and they operate like lenses in front of our eyes. They filter out aspects that don't agree with us, and zoom in on aspects that do agree with us. Thus beliefs are always self-verifying.

Limiting beliefs keep you locked in a negative state of mind, hindering you from going for new opportunities and life experiences, and wreaking havoc on your mental health. As I've said before, all of the success blockers are inextricably linked, so you may see some overlap, but it's important to discover the power of each of these success blockers as separate entities.

While your identity is the personality that you have created since you became part of the human world, you are first and foremost part of the sea of pure consciousness and have a unique blueprint programmed into your soul and spiritual self. Your soul sees no limits because it knows it's part of the field of infinite intelligence that is creative in nature. Therefore there is always a part of you that can see beyond what the human self is able to see. Your soul wants you to create more and knows that you're capable of it. However, your spiritual self does not exist as a separate part of you; it must coexist with your human identity – the self created while you joyride in this human body, also referred to as your ego. So having limiting beliefs goes against your true potential; and where your soul wants to fly, be free and create abundance, the limiting beliefs of the subconscious mind and the human self pull you back.

A limiting belief is like a tiny invisible monkey that sits on your shoulder, whispering in your ear all the reasons why you can't succeed. The crazy thing about these reasons is that most of them do not make sense logically – and your conscious mind uses reason and logic. However, it's not your conscious mind running the show, it's the irrational, illogical subconscious mind.

That's why we can logically say, 'Eating junk food is bad', and yet we still do it because, at a subconscious level, there's a whole different script playing out. The more you listen to those limiting beliefs, the bigger and more obnoxious they become! Before you know it, you're walking around with a 300-pound gorilla on your back, trying to achieve your goals while this hairy beast screams in your ear all the reasons why you're doomed to fail. This becomes part of the shitty committee we discussed earlier.

Let's have a look at some of the most funky, faulty beliefs that can trip us up along the way. See if any of them relate to you:

- I'm not young enough to be successful.
- I'm not old enough to be successful.
- I'm not thin enough to be successful.
- I'm not pretty enough to be successful.
- I don't have enough time to be successful.
- I don't have enough resources to be successful.
- I'm not smart enough to be successful.
- I don't have enough experience to be successful.
- I don't have enough money to be successful.
- I'm not talented/skilled enough to be successful.

Coaching note: recognize your own limiting beliefs

Become aware of any limiting beliefs you have that don't logically make sense and yet still have a strong hold on you. This will prove the concept shared earlier that your mind is made up of two components that are simply not working well together.

All of the above limiting beliefs have the word 'enough' in them, which is important as it's indicative of an invisible yardstick that we hold up for ourselves. If we boil them down, they can all be placed under one umbrella statement: 'I am not good enough.'

Coaching note: what do you need to be 'good enough' at?

When someone tells me they don't feel good enough to create what they want, my first answer is, 'Good enough compared to whom? Is there a specific person you are comparing yourself to? Or is it more a feeling that you get?'

What do you think you need to be good enough at in order to follow your heart's desires?

Why do most people think they are not 'good enough'?

As little children, we learn from our parents very early on that we get rewarded if we are 'good' and get in trouble if we are 'bad'. This moralistic approach to human behaviour is embedded in our society, and this perspective assumes that there are certain moral rules or standards that govern human behaviour, and that individuals should strive to adhere to these standards in order to be considered 'good'. Therefore actions that are seen as violating these principles are considered to be 'bad' or 'wrong'.

Since we cannot fend for ourselves as children, and since our primitive minds seek safety and survival, we learn that being 'good' equals love from our parents and, ultimately, safety and survival. This thing called 'goodness' is pleasing to the person who is feeding you and keeping you alive. Mummy will say, 'Good girl, I'm so proud of you' or 'Naughty boy, I'm so disappointed in you.' Children soon realize that pleasing the food-bringer is of the utmost importance because, in simple terms, no food equals starvation, which equals death. This way of thinking is instilled in children at an early age and is used as an invisible remote control, with each button able to direct children's behaviour.

Raise your hands if you've ever threatened to leave your tantruming child in a supermarket. My hands are raised, by the way! The reason this works so well in getting a child to comply is because we are inadvertently playing on children's innate and unconscious fear of abandonment and, ultimately, death. To a child, parental disapproval is a threat, and the thought of being left at the supermarket is enough for their mind to start seeing the abandonment that consequently leads to eventual death. Push one button on the remote and the child responds accordingly.

To add insult to injury, from childhood we are not only being judged by our parents and our teachers as to whether we are 'good enough', but we now add fictional characters into the mix. I hate to say it, but I have 100 per cent pulled out the 'Santa is watching you' card every single year in the run-up to Christmas, to ensure my children's compliance with being 'good'. Other people may use God or even the Easter bunny. Basically, children don't just believe they are always being judged 'good enough' or not by someone they know; there is also no escaping the judging eye of the man in the red suit with his Santa cam, or the omnipresent tooth fairy, checking in on perfectly cleaned teeth. This means that, as adults, we not only unconsciously fear judgement from things we can see, but also from things we can't.

The whole educational system is based on behavioural compliance with being 'good enough'. A child's work and behaviour are judged, and then the child is rewarded or punished accordingly (bad grades, suspension, expulsion). A system built on understanding human behaviour through the lens of credit, blame, pride and shame leaves people terrified of the embarrassment and humiliation of being judged poorly and disapproved of, and this script runs viciously in the background of our subconscious well into adulthood. As you can see, life hasn't made it very easy for us to ward this off!

When I was ten years old I moved from state school to private school and, quite honestly, the phrase 'fish out of water' doesn't do that justice. I was asked questions by my rather stern and cold form-tutor and so I answered. She called me a 'twit' and said, 'I don't know what school you've come from, but we don't do that here.' I wanted the world to suck me into the depths of its core.

That horrifying moment caused a level of trauma for me, and my mind did not process it properly. What happened left a tab open on the computer screen of my mind, leading to a mental webpage that said, 'This made me feel not good enough', which was added to every other open tab with other similar incidents in my life. Once a belief is created, it will continue to operate automatically in the background, serving as a reminder that you should not move forward.

This perspective on how our subconscious mind works, and why we have an epidemic of 'not good enough-ness', has really helped me understand the irrational behaviour not only of myself in the past, but also of my clients. I've always said that while most adults look like adults walking around and conversing with other adults, it doesn't take me very long (it's kinda my superpower!) to figure out what their limiting beliefs are, and how they are operating from a set of beliefs that their inner child is projecting – almost always stemming from feeling of not being good enough. Of course it's happening beyond any conscious awareness, but our subconscious mind works tirelessly to protect us from the feeling that not being good enough creates.

When we hold on to limiting beliefs, we feel stuck in our current circumstances and unable to move forward, putting our soul and our ego in constant conflict, which may in turn lead us to experience fear and anxiety about taking risks or pursuing our goals. Because, as children, we grow up understanding how to operate in life through this moralistic viewpoint, based on credit, blame, pride and shame (good girl/bad boy, I'm proud/disappointed in you), this becomes so deeply rooted in us that, even as adults, we operate at an unconscious level from the fear that if we aren't good enough, something bad will happen.

This has a significant impact on our ability to create success, because it leads us to doubt our abilities, question our worth and limit our potential for growth. Because we all have tabs left open on the computer screens of our minds, every time you experience a 'perceived threat' alert in life, your subconscious mind pulls up that open tab and you experience all those feelings again, resulting in you wanting to retreat to safety because you can't remove yourself from the emotional discomfort of the past.

So we inadvertently avoid challenges and opportunities that could potentially lead to success; and we fear taking action because the belief of not being good enough makes us wary of rejection or abandonment, setting off the sympathetic nervous system and causing all the physical symptoms of being in a threatening situation. Can you see how all of this is tying together? Basically, unless we dismantle the monkey and rescript our mind, we're fucked. Okay, now I'm being nearly as dramatic as the subconscious mind, but you can see that the power of our subconscious mind can truly stop us.

So how does this cause problems for us, as adults? Well, basically if we let that invisible monkey sit on our shoulder until it turns into the gorilla, and then we let it run the show, we might as well kiss goodbye to our dream life. So now you must be thinking, 'Noor, what do I do then?'

The power of Subconscious Rescripting®

One of the ways we can start to close the tab on the computer screen of the subconscious is through awareness, through understanding of the truth and through letting the subconscious mind know – through Subconscious Rescripting® – that it's no longer serving us to keep that tab open. By recognizing and addressing these beliefs, we can open up new possibilities for growth, achievement and fulfilment. So let's start with the belief that we are not good enough.

The word 'enough' indicates a measurement, and in this case it indicates that there is something missing: a gap between where you are and where you need to be. It's a belief that suggests that something 'good' needs to be added in order for you to reach the elusive goal of being 'enough'. But there is no person with a measuring tape waiting to see if you are 'good enough' for your dreams. You are *more than enough*, but awareness of what the gap is – and reframing it – is vital.

Being good enough is irrelevant. We don't need to be a good little girl or boy to be successful, so starting to untangle ourselves from this way of thinking is paramount. We need to remove the invisible yardstick that we are measuring ourselves against and recognize that it was instilled by our parents, trying to drum into us a moralistic way of behaving.

Sometimes it's also that we don't have the necessary skill sets **yet**. When I wanted to become a coach in 2014, I had no skill set and no experience. The thought process of not being good enough to make a successful career out of it was valid, as it was merely a dream. However, that sentence is incomplete. It wasn't that I wasn't 'good enough' to be a successful coach; it was that I wasn't good enough *yet* to be a successful coach.

Most of us are actually carrying beliefs that are not true. They feel true, but when we start to put those beliefs underneath a microscope and pull them apart, we can begin to see that they lack any weight. As humans, we are able to witness our thoughts – this is called metacognition – and, once we witness them, we are able to assess their validity and whether they are useful to us any more.

Having dysfunctional beliefs that cause us to stay stuck and prevent us moving towards our goals is the real enemy here. It's time now to look at all those limiting beliefs and teach your mind functional beliefs that will support you. As we have seen, I call this 'Subconscious Rescripting®'.

Coaching task: examine your beliefs

1. List all the beliefs you have that are limiting you from creating the success you desire.

2. Evaluate the consequences: consider how these beliefs have affected your life so far. What would happen if you were able to let go of them?

3. Fact-check: give each of the beliefs a reality check. Does it have any concrete evidence to back up its claims or is it simply spouting opinions like a political pundit on cable news? Are there facts that support this belief or is it based on subjective or anecdotal experiences? Look for evidence that contradicts the belief as well. You can say each belief out loud and ask yourself, 'Is this 100 per cent true?' You are here for a clear 'yes' or 'no' answer. It's either a fact or fiction.

4. Flip the script: I want you to flip the belief and ask yourself what the opposite of it is. If you were to create an empowering affirmation instead of a limiting belief, what would that look like?

5. Reframe the belief in a more positive and empowering way. For example, 'I may not have all the skills yet, but I'm capable of learning and growing', or 'I have valuable experience that I can bring to a new career path.' Add 'yet' to the end, where it is relevant, and try that out for size – this forces your mind to expand on the possibilities. Rephrase the sentence, putting in a new script that makes more sense to your adult mind: 'I don't have the necessary skills to build a successful coaching business *yet.*'

6. Take action: finally, take action to counteract the limiting belief. This might involve seeking out new opportunities, taking classes, training to develop new skills or seeking support and encouragement from others. When the subconscious mind knows it's safe to move forward, it starts to alter the feelings around that belief.

Remember, challenging limiting beliefs is an ongoing process – but just f*cking do it! It can take time and effort to shift your mindset, but with a day of persistence and a sprinkle of willingness to challenge your current subconscious scripts, you can overcome them and create a more fulfilling and successful story of your life. A successful life doesn't mean one that is absent of challenges. The reality is that we are all humans, and the misguided notion that we need to stay positive 24/7, 365 days a year, if we want to manifest our best life is, quite frankly, not only unrealistic, but completely unachievable.

Dealing with adversity

Whether we like it or not, we are going to be faced with situations in life that cause us to feel stressed, frustrated and overwhelmed and that will cause the monkey to reappear on our shoulder. When faced with such events, we may find ourselves getting sucked into the emotional drama, and our thoughts may take hold and we are off down the negative rabbit hole quicker than the White Rabbit can say, 'I'm late! I'm late! I'm late!'

That's why we need to understand that it's okay to have negative thoughts and be affected by everyday life, but it's *how* we deal with them that will make us the master of our vibration.

Imagine for a moment that you are on a flight to luscious, magical, sunny Hawaii. The plane is heading straight there, and you feel so good and so aligned on this journey. You are excited because the vision of your destination, with its powder-white sand and swishing palm trees, is embedded in your mind's eye. Then suddenly the seatbelt light goes on and the plane begins to shudder, and you feel the wrath of dreaded turbulence as the pilot announces something unexpected. 'Due to unforeseen circumstances . . .' he bellows over the tannoy, 'the plane is now headed to Antarctica.'

'What the actual—!'

Suddenly the dream of warm sun and sipping Mai Tais goes out of the window as you head for freezing-cold Antarctica.

When we have a vision for our lives, our goals mapped out and are moving with flow and grace, none of us likes to feel turbulence along the way. Moreover, we hate a diversion, because we all desire a smooth journey. However, in life sometimes the shit hits the fan, something goes wrong and we are like, 'Oh, man, did that actually just happen?'

Let's be frank: Antarctica is not built for holidaymakers; it's cold, there are no nice hotels and while you could build an igloo there, you would rather not. The great thing is that the plane that unexpectedly took you there, and the pilot who flew you, are still both there. You have the choice to get back on the plane and ask the pilot to fly you to Hawaii. Or you can stay in the cold atmosphere of Antarctica. You can sit and wallow in your misery, bask in victim mentality, stay stuck with no solutions, allowing yourself to get wrapped in fear, anger and stress . . . or you can get back on the plane and instruct the pilot to fly you to Hawaii.

We can choose at any time – we have that ability. Sometimes it seems like a great idea to stay in a space where you are feeling pain, anger, resentment, jealousy or sadness. There's nothing wrong with you feeling those things, if that's what you are choosing. It's when you feel that you have no control over the matter that you are in a helpless situation. If you desire to wallow in your misery, who am I to stop you? It's your life and it's your choice! It's also your decision to pick yourself up, understand the data the situation is giving you and recalibrate your emotions, so that you can get back on track with manifesting what you desire.

So what happens when you go off-piste and something knocks you from your vibrational high? How do you get back to being Tuned in to Universe FM? Is it even possible not to sweat the small stuff? I say 'yes'. Your dream life requires you to become an energetic match for it, and that means you need to decide if you allow the small shit in life to be what breaks you down. You cannot be beaten by one negative thought – it's just a thought!

When I was at university I and my best friend Lucy had a contemplation corner. Whenever we felt 'off', we would play sad music, sit in the contemplation corner and feel sorry for ourselves. But for every moment you stay in Antarctica freezing your ass off, or allow contemplation to consume you in a designated corner, you miss out on the magic of Hawaii. You don't ever get those moments back, because time is the only thing in finite supply to us humans. Will you spend it feeling mad, sad and plonked in the contemplation corner, surrounded by snotty tissues, or moving towards sunnier shores?

So how do you get back on the plane and on your way to Hawaii quickly? The first thing you can do is neutralize your thoughts, which in turn helps to regulate the nervous system and the emotions you are feeling. Neutralizing your thoughts doesn't mean that you are trying to go from grief to joy in five seconds; it's about shifting your energy slightly to a more neutral position, to help your energy find its way back to its happy place. It's about coming back to the present moment and recognizing that you do not need to suffer. Pain is physical, suffering is mental and a result of our thoughts – nothing more. It's about witnessing your thoughts and calling them out for the bullshit they are.

You should not berate yourself for feeling the way you do. It's bad enough feeling sad, without adding to the mix feeling mad about being sad. And then feeling guilty about being mad about being sad! You'll find yourself lost down the alleyways that I talked of earlier, if you let these emotions start spiralling. Allow yourself to feel it. It's okay to be mad, to be sad, to feel frustrated – you are only human. It's when we compound that with judgement that we get stuck in the proverbial mud.

Next, I want you to name the emotion you are feeling and then ask yourself, 'What thought is creating that feeling?' Witness that thought! That thought isn't *who* you truly are; that thought is a response to something. What are your thoughts and feelings trying to tell you at this moment about what you are experiencing?

When we take time to understand the meaning of the data coming in, we can become an observer, rather than be in the middle of the boxing ring being smashed to pieces by our thoughts and feelings.

Next, breathe; yes, breathing is proven to help switch on the parasympathetic nervous system and take you out of fight-or-flight mode.

Lastly, ask yourself what thoughts would make you feel a bit better. It doesn't need to make you feel like you are on cloud nine, but what thoughts will take you one step closer to peace? One of the best ways I am able to shift out of a funk is by pivoting my perspective. I'm looking for the lesson, looking for the good, accepting that the situation is happening to me for the betterment of myself. It's honestly one of the easiest ways for me to move out of a funk and into a happier place.

Moving your attention to something different, rather than focusing on the negative experience, begins to dilute the power of that experience, allowing it to wash over you. That's why I love to switch my mind to what I'm grateful for. Switching my focus to gratitude is one of the simplest, yet most powerful tools that I use when something gets under my skin. Feelings aren't permanent, they pass; they are emotions that are energy in motion, and they will keep moving if we don't put up such a fight to keep them there. You get to choose how you respond and how you move through this experience that your body is having.

So as we close this conversation about limiting beliefs, I want to remind you of a powerful truth: you are *more than good enough*. In moments of doubt, remember that your worth is not defined by external validation or the opinions of others. It is rooted in the essence of who you are, in your unique gifts, talents and passions. You are a f*cking miracle, so:

- Embrace your imperfections.
- Embrace your failures.
- Embrace your strengths.
- Embrace the knowledge that your mind is there to help you, but that sometimes it gets the wrong memo and it's your job to reroute.

Remember that Subconscious Rescripting® is a powerful tool.

You can start to rewire your mind and regulate your nervous system, and you can access this in my programmes and memberships. And whenever that monkey pops up on your shoulder, turn your head and whisper gently in its ear that you are in charge, breathe and watch the monkey disappear.

Mastering your thoughts, emotions and vibration takes practice, but it's a practice that will result in huge pay-offs for your life and your success. So taking the time to become the master of your thoughts and feelings will truly make you one of the most successful humans on this planet.

16.

Success Blocker #4: Negative self-image

Complete the sentence 'I am my own worst . . .'

When I asked this in front of 300 people in a packed room at one of my live events, the whole room quickly chimed in within seconds, in perfect unison, 'ENEMY!'

It's a hugely damaging concept that is so widely accepted that within milliseconds we can read it off like a script embedded in our psyche. When we believe that we are our worst enemy, how the hell are we meant to trust ourselves to create our best life? As I shared in the previous chapter, it's like that invisible monkey sitting on our shoulder, criticizing us.

Most psychologists agree that the roots of our inner critics are to be found in childhood. That's why in this chapter we are going to examine the fourth success blocker and the concept of self-image, and how a negative self-image is something we need to understand and overcome. I'm not going to be referring to your physical self-image. While the debate about physical self-image is certainly of great importance – with statistics showing the adverse effects, particularly among women – for the purposes of this book I want to talk about your *inner* self-image, beyond your physical appearance. It's the way you view yourself and what you are capable of.

Let's take a moment to address the word 'self', which makes up half of the word 'your*self*'. I want for a moment to think about the word 'self'. The self appears to be separate from us. I've discussed earlier that there is a lack of alignment between the conscious and subconscious mind, and this shows up in our language patterns. People often say, 'I don't like myself', 'I sabotage myself' or 'I'm my own worst enemy.' These language patterns point to a disconnect between the two facets of the mind – the 'I' and the 'self' – which appear to be operating independently, each with its own agenda.

The way I like to view this is that the self is not the true essence of you, at a soul level. It's not the you that is made of magical spiritual stardust and composed with perfection by an infinite intelligence. It's the part of you that was manufactured so you could partake in the human world. Your self holds all the beliefs and conditioning that we have explored multiple times in this book already. What I'd like to focus on in this chapter is how you see yourself and how you perceive others seeing you, which is hindering you from moving towards the vision for your life.

Your self-image can be very positive, giving you confidence in your thoughts and actions. Conversely, it can be negative, making you doubtful of your capabilities and ideas. Think about the story of your life so far. Do you see yourself as successful – someone who is the hero of your story – or do you see yourself as a victim?

When someone is suffering from a negative self-image, their symptoms are focusing on their own weaknesses and their distorting faults and imperfections. That's when that invisible critical monkey comes out to play and can be a rather cruel and self-flagellating force, which punishes and tyrannizes them. So how do you recognize your inner critic?

Let's look at some of the things that your inner critic might say:

- What's the matter with you?
- Why do you keep trying? You'll never be good at it.
- You're not as attractive/pretty/slim as other people.
- You need to be perfect or no one will like you.
- Why can't you be like them?

How we think about ourselves affects how we feel about ourselves, and how we interact with others and the world around us. When we don't view ourselves as the miraculous human we are, with unique strengths and talents and the ability to contribute to the world in our own unique way, we allow this inner critic to judge us, which can be pretty destructive to our self-esteem.

Therefore self-image has a lot to do with self-esteem, which can also be thought of as self-confidence and how we see the value that we have to offer to the world around us. When we have low self-esteem, we don't like or value ourselves as a person. We struggle to assert ourselves and make decisions. We struggle to recognize our strengths, and we can't get over past mistakes without blaming ourselves unfairly. We may deem ourselves unworthy and expect the world to see us that way, too.

As we have discussed previously, a child depends completely on its parents for survival, and the conscious acknowledgement and rebuttal of parents' unfairness, cruelty or incompetence is simply too much for a child to combat, as it's a threat to their survival. Therefore it is much safer for a child to turn the criticism inwards rather than outwards, and to blame the 'self' for their suffering. So while the inner critic was originally there to help, as a sensible survival mechanism, it can be a truly debilitating handicap when we are adults.

We talked about limiting beliefs in the last chapter, and if we have beliefs that we are unlovable – or bad, evil, not good enough, ugly, incompetent, stupid or flawed in other ways – then our inner critic will constantly broadcast these messages to us, contributing to us viewing ourselves negatively. As you can see, our limiting beliefs and self-image are not mutually exclusive.

In order for us to manifest success, I truly believe that we need to see ourselves through a different lens. Imagine how your best friend, or someone else who loves you, sees you. We need to learn to love ourselves in exactly the same way. Showing kindness to yourself, believing that you matter and that you deserve happiness is crucial for your future.

Why do I think self-image is significant for creating success, particularly when it comes to building a thriving business? Because, as I've said, creating success requires you to be clear on the vision of your life, have an identity that matches it and a commitment to taking inspired action.

- If you don't see yourself as capable of creating what you want . . .
- If you aren't able to view yourself as a happy, healthy person . . .
- If you don't believe that you are at least somewhat close to your ideal version of yourself . . .

then it's going to be very difficult to take action towards creating what you want.

If you are a business owner, you need to see yourself in the role of a badass CEO who runs a successful business, instead of someone just trying to make a bit of cash on the side, otherwise you will be a statistic on the 'businesses that failed this year' list. Why? Because one of the saddest reasons for someone not going for what they want is that they feel a fraud or imposter; yes, the good old imposter syndrome is about as bad as a bout of herpes.

My clients often say they feel that they are 'faking it' or are not deserving of success. They downplay their achievements, compare themselves unfavourably to others and experience intense anxiety or fear at being discovered as a fraud. This can lead to self-doubt, stress and a constant need to prove themselves.

Whenever someone feels like an imposter, I remind them that this is a great thing as it means they are stepping outside their comfort zone. In your comfort zone you have the same thoughts and results in life, and thus it's natural to feel afraid as your mind begins to stretch from where you are to the next level of your reality. When you step outside your comfy zone, you experience new pastures and, yes, you will feel like an imposter, because you're now in the 'not so comfy' parts of you world! It's like wearing in new shoes – it gives you blisters to start with, but then they fit like a dream.

Imposter syndrome is actually common among people who are continually learning and developing their skills. It signifies that you have a growth mindset and are open to new challenges and opportunities. Embracing the discomfort of imposter syndrome can lead to personal and professional growth as you strive to expand your knowledge and capabilities.

Simply remind your mind that you are the best person for the job, and commit to becoming better and better at whatever you're doing. The more competent you get, the more confident you will become, and that imposter feeling will quickly begin to dissipate.

Coaching note: how do others see you?

Take a moment to imagine yourself as the *best* version of yourself, exuding confidence. Think about how that version of you is showing up in the world. Consider how you feel about that version of yourself. Think about how others *see* you.

Turning your inner critic into your inner coach

One of the best ways we can start to see ourselves through positive eyes is to go to those who love us most. This may be a hard task, but I want you to ask those people what they love about you. I want you to write all their answers down and allow yourself to observe that the way you see yourself is often vastly different when you are viewed through the lens of love.

Second, I want you to learn how you can catch the inner critic and turn it into your inner coach. It is necessary to catch that critic in order to build and maintain self-esteem. The next time you find yourself in a cycle of negative thoughts, take a minute to tune into your inner critic. What kinds of things are you saying? When are automatic thoughts most likely to come up? How long does this experience last?

I want you to write your answers down and keep a log. Use a journal to note down whenever you engage with your inner critic's voice. As the first step in overriding the power of this destructive voice that is affecting your self-image, I'd like you to say out loud,

'Not useful. Cut that noise down!' You may look as if you have Tourette's syndrome, but this is a very powerful tool.

In that moment your job is to consciously say out loud three things about you that are amazing, and which oppose that negative thought. Imagine that you are in a court of law defending your most important client: that's the job you need to do at this moment, and you can start each of the three sentences with 'I'm great because . . .'

Every day that you strive towards your dreams and goals, you will inevitably grow your self-esteem, and your self-image will begin to improve – it is a marathon, not a sprint, people! Every time you attain a milestone, congratulate yourself and note that milestone down. This builds a solid foundation of self-esteem and self-confidence and moves you closer to that success. As you begin to recognize your ability to get where you desire, your confidence will grow and the more you will view yourself as the badass that I know you are.

17

Success Blocker #5: Out of alignment

Can you believe that we are now going to tackle the fifth and final success blocker that is potentially coming between you and your dream life? Everything you've ever wanted is within reaching distance, but let's talk about this buzzword in the coaching and spiritual world: 'alignment'.

Alignment feels like dancing to the beat of your own drum without caring who's watching. It's when your mind, body and soul are all singing in perfect harmony and you feel like you're in a state of flow. It's like being a superhero with a power suit that perfectly fits you, allowing you to tackle any challenge with ease and grace. When we are aligned, our conscious desires and subconscious beliefs are speaking the same language, understand each other perfectly and are working in unison to bring us closer to our dreams. Alignment is the easy straight road to Success-ville.

That's why the fifth and final culprit that will block you from hooking up with success is being 'out of alignment'. This feels like driving a car with the wheels pointing in different directions, making it difficult to steer it in the right way. Basically, being out of alignment leaves you feeling frustrated and stuck.

The first part of getting aligned is making sure that your conscious desires about what you want to create are singing to the same tune as your subconscious beliefs. If these two aren't harmonizing together, then the result will sound like me singing in the shower – and I can assure you that sounds more like a dying dog than Adele.

Through Subconscious Rescripting® we can teach our unconscious mind not to automatically go to a fight-or-flight response, and to close down the tabs of past experiences that are acting as a trigger in our current lives. If you recall, in earlier chapters I explained that when things happen to us as children, the mind does not always process them correctly and since the mind is prone to a data-processing dysfunction, these experiences are left like open tabs in our mind. If we experience anything structurally similar to that past experience, the mind will perceive a threat and we automatically have a primitive response in order to protect ourselves.

Once we close down past tabs in our minds, this saves energy so that our bodies can use it elsewhere, but it also means that we aren't unnecessarily feeling scared, which is of course the number-one blocker; being scared and anxious also uses a lot of unnecessary energy.

When we can regulate our nervous system and thus our energy, we can teach our minds new beliefs and can harness the power of neuroplasticity to rewire those new thoughts that are conducive to us moving forward. Thus managing our energy and becoming aligned are advantageous in helping us achieve success.

The route to Success-ville

What I want to delve into now is the route you decide to take to get where you want to be: your very own Success-ville. You see, how we *do* things as humans is very important, because everything we do either elevates or depletes our vital energy. As unique beings, there are many different ways in which each of us can do things in order to achieve the results we want.

Let's say you decide on an impromptu holiday with your friends to Spain and the travel agent says, 'What mode of transport would you like to take?' She explains that you have the choice between a coach, a plane and a train. They will all get you where you need to go, but each journey and route will differ, and deciding which route is best suited to *you* is where the magic of alignment lies.

And just as there are different ways to get to your Spanish holiday, so there are many different ways to make money, to exercise, to find a partner and to build wealth. The road to Success-ville for one person will be completely different from that of another person. Aligning with the route that's best for you will make that journey to Success-ville feel like the smoothest road trip in a beautiful vintage Mustang, with your favourite tunes blaring out. The issue is that most people simply never understand this and go through their entire lives travelling down the bumpy road with a shitload of potholes in a 1980s Yugo.

When we try to get to a destination using a metaphorical mode of transport or a hypothetical route that isn't aligned with us, beware: there will be consequences! While there are different ways to create abundance and success in your life, some of the ways will feel good to you and others will seem clunky and will cause you resistance.

After my fourth child was born, I mentioned to a friend of mine that I wanted to get back to working out. She excitedly suggested several times joining her at these really intense workout classes and tried to sell it to me by saying, 'It's so hard that you will be so sweaty, and people even throw up!'

When I heard that, I wanted to run for the hills, whereas for someone else it might have felt like an exciting way to spend a Sunday morning. If I had forced myself to do that class, my subconscious mind would have worked even harder to dissuade me from doing exercise in the future, because feeling like I want to throw up is not a vibe for me. Because our minds like us to do what it feels good to do, it would have pushed me further away from my goals of working out.

If you try to lose weight by running, but hate doing it, how long do you think you will stick at it? It's the same with making money. If you want to make money and I suggested you do that by becoming an accountant, but you despise numbers, is that something you could endure long-term? I'd say no. That's why alignment is a bespoke and personal journey of connection with your own soul for whatever feels good to *you*. *Having a means to an end that isn't a joyful or fulfilling experience doesn't make for a successful or fulfilling existence.*

My business selling products made me money, which gave me freedom, but after eighteen months and with the business honey-moon over, I couldn't shake the feeling that I was meant for coaching. My heart wasn't in selling products. Why? First, I never ever had a dream of having a multimillion-pound product brand. I had set up the business to make some extra money, so that I could be a stay-at-home mum. It served that purpose for eighteen months, but was out of alignment with who I was at my core, because my purpose was to help others. I tried to ignore the inner calling of my soul and stick at the products business because, as humans, we are taught that we shouldn't 'give up'. But I felt as if my soul was contracting.

Sometimes one thing we do runs its course, and we need that other 'thing' to help us grow and evolve. Following our soul's call-ing isn't giving up. While at school, our lives are all geared towards picking *one* career to stick with, till death do us part. I believe that, as entrepreneurs who are full of creative ideas, evolution happens and we find our way down different paths. I'm not suggesting that you keep changing ideas every week and trying something new every month, but honour your soul's calling and understand that 'pushing' to stick with something that doesn't feel good any more is not the answer, just for the sake of saving face.

The strategy that you take to get where you want to be *matters*, unless you like feeling clunky and resistant along the way. The con-sequence of chronic misalignment is that people end up getting burnt out. They are using their energy against themselves and it causes them to frazzle. Those things literally become energy leaks in our lives and deplete us. When we do things that bring us joy, they generate energy instead of draining us.

Coaching note: are you expanding or contracting?

Does what you are doing make you feel expansive or contracting? Think about a cute baby puppy or someone you love dearly – that is the feeling of expansion. Now think about someone you dislike or a situation that makes you feel really sad – that is the feeling of contracting. When we are in alignment, we feel expansion!

Following the flow

When we have the right strategy, we find ourselves in a state of flow. The phrase 'flow state' describes a mental state in which someone is completely focused on a single task or activity.

For example, when I came to write this book and I got into a state of flow, I could write for what seemed like a minute and yet an hour had gone by. That's because I had accessed a mental state where I could get more shit done – it's like tapping into a creative energy that almost feels like it's outside yourself. When I access flow states, it usually means that I'm doing the right things in my life. Some people refer to this as 'being in the zone'; it's when you can direct all your attention towards a task and you don't experience many thoughts about yourself or your performance.

When we are not in alignment, getting into this flow state is harder. I can only really get into the zone when I am in alignment with what I am doing and how I'm doing it.

So how do we get our energy aligned and tap into the right strategy for us as individuals? Great question. First, it's by really trusting your intuition to guide you to align with the actions that feel right for you. It's about connecting and listening to your internal guidance system, instead of always thinking about a logical plan of action. This is hard for humans, as we are taught to be logical rather than intuitive. We are taught at school to memorize answers, which then determine how clever we are, thereby using our logical brain rather than our creative mind and our intuition.

My daughter Layla-Rose is super-artistic and talented when it comes to drawing, and spends hours in a flow state with her pencils and notepad. The school recently announced there was an art competition and she was so excited to enter. 'What shall I draw?' she asked. She started reeling off loads of ideas, but I could hear something that worried me. The brief was to draw something that had a meaning to it, but her logical brain was trying to think about what she 'should' draw to impress the school and to win.

I stopped her and said, 'Stop thinking about what you would prefer [logical brain trying to figure out how to win], take a step back and allow your intuition to guide you to draw something that *means* something to you and that you would love to do.' I wanted her to enjoy the process, and wished to teach her to tap into her internal guidance system. 'The universe has your back, baby girl, and it isn't about winning. But if you draw something with meaning, you will enjoy it and it will make the impact it needs to make on whoever sees it,' I told her.

Layla-Rose came back to me about twenty minutes later with a page of annotations. She was excited and giddy, and I knew she was harnessing the flow state. She said, 'Oh my goodness, I have an amazing idea!' An idea is the gift of your intuition and universal intelligence. Whenever I get a great idea, it can usually be felt in my body and in accompanying physical symptoms, such as goosebumps. These are always the bolts of inspiration that we should follow.

Coaching note: follow the path of least resistance

Think about the strategies and tactics you are currently using in your life and/or business. How do they make you feel? Drained or excited? Check in with that for a moment.

Make the journey of success count. Choose wisely how you execute things and if you need to pivot, that's completely okay. Follow the path of least resistance and you will get to your destination with far more ease and flow.

When we work with our strengths, our values, our likes and our passions, we can enjoy every part of the journey of getting where we want to be, and this also helps us play the long game in creating what we want. When our soul's calling is honoured by the ego, and our ego is on board to help, we are in alignment. When our conscious desires and subconscious beliefs are not conflicting, we are in alignment. When we find the best way for us, as individuals, to get where we want to go, then we are harnessing the natural flow of energy that will support us in moving towards that broader vision.

Curating your energy

Committing to the curation of our energy means becoming self-aware on a daily basis when things don't feel good and recalibrating that. Keeping our energy in check also means thinking about how the environment in which we wish to do things is conducive to our success. A few months ago I had this overpowering urge to rearrange my whole office. I had so many things I needed to do that day, but I couldn't help feeling that I needed a shift in the energy in my work-space. I had been reading up about Feng Shui and how I could apply it to the new house that we were building, and one of the things that stood out to me was the advice never to put an office desk against a wall, as it stops the flow of energy of abundance. As I looked at my desk, plonked right up against a wall, I couldn't help feeling the urge to move it!

Whether that's true or not, there's undoubtedly a nice feeling that you get when you rearrange items in a room. When a cluttered space becomes clear, it's quite extraordinary how that space can make you feel. I'll be honest: I'm no domestic goddess, and being clean, tidy and organized is not something that comes naturally to me. I love everything looking tidy and organized, but I simply don't enjoy the process of getting there. I'd much rather spend my time doing other things. However, I cannot deny the peace that comes from a decluttered space, and the feeling of motivation that I get from soaking up a newly tidied space feels *good*.

When it comes to manifesting, feeling good is the key, so that's why the space in which I'm creating my dream life needs to make me feel good. This is a conscious curation of energy. When we live in disorganization and mess, this can cause an energy leak, because instead of being productive and focusing on the task in hand, our minds wander and become fixated on a pile of paperwork or the clothes in the corner. Instead of doing what we need to do to get things done, we end up forcing our brains to focus on what is annoying us. Our environment really does have an impact on our success.

Decluttering has been talked about heavily in the manifestation space, and I do believe there is merit to it. Whether you decide to go full Marie Kondo on your life or just fancy a spruce-up, be mindful of your 'creative' space – also known as your office space. If you aren't in business, try to find a space in your home that is your area for creating your dream life. You can put your vision board there, or perhaps you love a crystal, like me, and can have this as your space to hang out and think, and journal about your new life or read books like this one!

Energy leaks

Everything in life – all the people, our experiences and our choices – either puts wind in our sails or depletes us of energy; when it depletes us, this is an energy leak.

After all, we are spiritual beings made of energy, so meticulous awareness of what causes us to drain of energy, versus generating energy, is important to us in creating our most successful life. As a business owner, I find certain tasks contracting and arduous. I call these 'shit sandwich' tasks. They still need to be done, but recognizing that I do not need to be the one doing them is very powerful. Delegating the 'shit sandwich' tasks means you can focus on being in your zone of genius, and on feeling aligned with your strategy.

Anything that causes you to feel less than peaceful, happy and content is an energy leak, and you need to plug that *pronto*. Do not be scared to put fierce boundaries in place, and to keep shedding anything that does not serve you. This means everything to do with your body, your friends, your work, your environment and even your food choices.

If you walk around your house and something 'bugs' you, fix that energy leak. If you're going about your daily life and something feels draining, stop it. It really is as simple as that. It may not be easy, but I promise you it will be the best and most liberating thing you ever do.

Coaching task: energy-leak reconnaissance

For your second coaching-related topic in this chapter, I want you to do an *energy-leak reconnaissance*. Think about the things in your life that are making you feel funky – and not funky in a *Saturday Night Fever* dancing kinda way, but in a 'this doesn't feel right and is messing with my mojo' kind of way. Think about how you are doing things in your life, who you are hanging out with and what your environments are like. Begin to become aware of what needs to change so that you feel more aligned and can bring joy to your life each day. You can use the handy worksheet at www.thisisyourdream. com/success to help you. Thank me later!

When you start plugging your energy leaks, you will be incredibly surprised by how much better you feel – it's almost like a lightness that comes over you. Commit to this practice of plugging energy leaks in your life and I promise it will be a game-changer.

18

Success leaves clues

I'm incredibly excited that you have got to this point in the book – now you truly understand what could be blocking you and have started to take steps to overcome it. In my courses and member-ships, which you can check out at www.thisisyourdream.com/workwithme, you can learn more about how to smash through these blockers so that you can break through in life and in business.

As we start to come towards the end of our journey together, I thought it would be good to shift the gears from what is block-ing you to what can help accelerate your success. I want to show how you can take everything we have done so far and ramp it up, so that you can really create a level of personal mastery that will lead you to manifest your dreams even quicker.

The year 2014 was the first year that I began my journey of per-sonal development. My mum had recently been recruited to a network marketing company, and she was loving it. She seemed so different, so positive and full of life. As a result, she also became interested in personal development and, slowly but surely, the study in her house began to fill with positive-thinking books and old-school CDs in huge plastic containers.

I had taken a sales job while figuring out what the fuck to do with my life, and it involved a lot of travel. Because of the amount of time I spent in my car, I decided to borrow a couple of my mum's audio CDs. I felt this pull towards two authors: one was Jim Rohn (who was dead by then) and the other was Darren Hardy. I became obsessed with learning how to be successful and how to change my life, and with each mile I spent driving to potential clients' homes, I absorbed powerful words from my first two mentors.

One of the first life-changing concepts I learned from Darren was that of the compound effect, and I became immersed in listening to him talk about the power of momentum. The compound effect is the principle of reaping great rewards from a series of small, but smart choices. While the benefits of the compound effect are massive, the steps taken can sometimes feel insignificant. They offer few to no immediate results, so many people negate its power.

'Small, smart choices + consistency + time = radical difference,' Darren would say through my car speakers. In a world where we are conditioned for immediate gratification, this was a very different way of thinking for me. As humans, we love to know how to lose ten pounds in ten minutes, find the love of our lives after one date, make one million pounds overnight, and so on. Commitment takes so much effort!

One example that blew my twenty-eight-year-old mind was how a penny that doubles in value every day for thirty-one days is worth more than ten million. At twenty days it is still worth a small £5,243, but on day thirty-one, it's a whopping £10,737,418.20. Most of the gain happens not at once, but towards the end. That's the magic of the compound effect – something that most people never stick around long enough to appreciate.

We aren't taught about the power of momentum and compound interest, and so when we don't see immediate results in our lives or business we get disheartened and lose faith. But we need to understand that when we compound small but smart choices in the direction of that which we wish to achieve, we gain something called momentum.

Momentum

Learning how to build momentum is one of the first steps towards finding success in life, because momentum is a powerful force propelling you towards your dreams; it is the force created by a moving object – aka *you*. I read once that it takes more fuel for a plane to take off than it does for the whole journey, and I resonate with this. Starting something new, such as a business, can feel like it takes so much energy, and that is why the early days of doing anything new can feel draining. Most people find this phase so taxing that they give up, but this is detrimental. I believe those early days are crucial and, if you lose momentum, it can feel ten times harder to get back on track, which is why committing to the bigger picture is so important.

I suggest that in order to keep momentum going in anything, you should try and do a little bit of whatever it is that you need to do each day. The reality is that once you have the force of momentum behind you in any area of your life, you want to ride that wave like you are a pro-surfer at Bondi. By building momentum, you are creating a world in which you are more productive, more effective and more efficient. When you get into the flow of things it becomes second nature, but when you take three weeks off from the gym for Christmas and stuff your gob with mince pies, getting back into it when the New Year starts feels like a huge effort.

Once you get going – even just a little bit – it's so much easier to keep going. The more small steps you take, the more momentum you build and the more comfortable you will be doing that activity or task, and the more productive and effective you will be.

Take non-negotiable action every single day, even if it's only for twenty minutes, until you start getting some real traction. Become dedicated to whatever it is you want to achieve and, before you know it, after one week you will have been productive for just over two hours. It all adds up, and making it a routine will help embed it as a habit. That way, you can begin to increase the number with far more ease once it's become part of your life.

Coaching note: the force of momentum

Think about any time when you've started something, such as a workout routine. Think about the tasks you have been successful at versus those you have given up on. What are the differences? You will notice that when you made something a habit because you allowed momentum to gather, you were more likely to stick at it and get results.

Discipline = freedom

One of the easiest ways to get momentum is by planning things efficiently. One of my mentors taught me in my early days that discipline is actually freedom, and it wasn't till I started planning out my days, weeks and months diligently that I finally knew exactly what he meant.

It takes a lot more time planning, thinking and trying to execute things in *reaction* to your life rather than proactively planning what you need to do and then taking action according to that plan. The latter means that you can naturally ride the wave of momentum, rather than spending time figuring out what the hell to do. When we can free our minds up because we have planned what we need to do, we then have time when our brains have the opportunity to tap into creativity and get new ideas and inspiration. Our brains need time off for them to work optimally.

Getting clear on your yearly vision, monthly goals and daily steps, and marking them all in your planner, means that you know where you want to go and how to get there more effectively. So plan out your week at the start, blocking out your days into chunks of times and certain activities, and prioritize to-do lists. This will help you have a clear head, moving forward, and will remove the overwhelm that 'What the heck shall I do?' can bring. Such clarity sets the internal compass in motion towards getting results, as has been shown in many studies into how to set goals and achieve them.

As the mother of four children, who seems to receive an exponentially large list of school activities on a weekly basis, planning my life properly sometimes feels like a military expedition. It takes real discipline to get everything done that I need to, but also an awareness of what my priorities actually are, when it comes to my business and my life. Sometimes this involves making hard decisions so that I can create the success I desire.

Each day I look at my to-do list and ask myself, 'What are my top three priorities?' And by that I mean what are the top three things I should do that will move my life forward, in the direction of my dreams? This discernment helps to keep my mind clear and focused and able to execute tasks effectively.

Hard decisions for an easy life

As you begin to grow in your life, you will find that you are faced with opportunities for growth that may require making hard decisions in order to protect your energy and propel your growth, not stunt it. I once read that one of the best traits of the most successful people is making decisions, even if they're not 100 per cent sure it's the right one. Because *not* making a decision is a sure-fire way to kill momentum. Sometimes that decision feels hard – like saying no to someone, which will bring up lots of emotions for the people-pleasers out there. Saying no, even if the decision is hard, literally creates space in your life for the *new*.

Coaching note: keep moving

Think about the relief you feel after you've made a decision, even if it was hard. Maybe the relief did not come immediately, but it always comes. Now think of a decision that you need to make – sense how that feels in your body. That feeling is restricting the natural flow of energy and keeps you in a lower vibrational state, which is why it's important to keep moving!

The paralysis of indecision

Successful people will make a decision so that they move forward, because nothing feels as paralysing as indecision! *Sit with that sentence.* Think about a time when you needed to make a decision and couldn't figure it out – the interim while you decide can be mentally agonizing. Sometimes I'll be planning a trip and I can't decide where to go, or spend hours trawling through reviews to figure out the best place and still find myself not picking. That stuckness takes away from the fact that I'm trying to plan something wonderful and causes me mental discomfort. Moving quickly out of that sticky state feels like a relief and is liberating, and while there will be levels of discomfort when making hard decisions other than simply 'Where shall we stay on holiday?', it's important to recognize that being okay with discomfort is part of our growth.

Learn to make decisions, even if you're not 100 per cent sure they are right. The more in tune with your own intuition you become, the more you will trust those decisions. And making hard decisions does get easier, the more you accept that it's part of becoming a bigger version of yourself.

In addition, decision-making should not be a purely mental job. Sit down and write everything out. Trying to muddle through stuff in your mind alone leads to overwhelm. See it in black and white on paper, then take some time to sit by yourself and ask, 'What do I truly want to do?'

Reflect on the positive effects of making a decision, and weigh them up against the consequences of *not* making a decision. If you stay as you are, how will that affect you? Sit in silence and allow yourself to feel in your body and to hear what your inner guidance is trying to tell you. Trust that guidance, if it feels good inside you. Sense in your body what each decision feels like, and revisit it daily until you feel that it's correct. And set yourself a deadline to have finalized a decision, so that you aren't stuck in 'decision limbo', feeling the stuckness.

Raising your standards

My daughter intermittently complains that her legs ache, and I know these are growing pains. And in the same way that we have these pains as children, we have them as we break through different levels of our lives. We will feel discomfort when we expand to new horizons and grow as human beings, and one of the things I love to tell myself as I go through such growing pains is, 'This is happening for my betterment.' Being able to pivot my perspective from 'Oh, man, this is shit' to 'This is going to help me break through the next glass ceiling' gives me reassurance that, on the other side of the stickiness, there is light.

I once heard someone say that in life you don't get what you want – you get what you tolerate. The successful people I know simply don't tolerate the shit that most people accept. They have raised the standards of what they expect for their lives, for their family, their friends, their vocations and their health. We can all do better if we want to, in all areas of our lives, and this continuing desire for growth and improvement is truly exciting.

Raising your standards about what you expect from yourself and others – even from seemingly meaningless tasks, such as keeping your office space or home tidy, to the relationship dynamics you are willing to accept – makes a huge difference to your overall lifetime experience.

I've run my business with a small team for the best part of the last decade. One of the hardest decisions, when running a business, is letting go of team members who are not performing to the standard you need. But by identifying what the energy leaks in my life were, I was able to address them – and my team was one of those leaks. The same goes for friends who you know aren't right for you; for relationships that you are staying in, even though they are toxic; and for jobs that you cling to, even when they drain you each day.

When I'm involved in any sort of relationship that isn't good for me, and yet I stay, I notice that I operate from a very different part of myself. When I've been in romantic relationships that haven't been right for me, I feel anxious and I get frustrated and behave in ways that make me feel pretty ashamed. When I have team members that I've kept on who weren't doing their job correctly, yet I retained them out of a sense of guilt, I then found everything they did wrong afterwards was amplified, because there was this guilt running in the background that caused me a constricting feeling.

The more you avoid hard decisions, the more you get stuck in this emotionally crunchy space. However, the more you choose to raise your own standards and make hard decisions in order to do that, the more you will start to feel empowered. And this will be the catalyst for you moving closer to the vision of your life on your own terms.

It's hard to say to friends or people you love that you think it's better that you part ways, but one element of raising your standards means that you are choosing *more* for you. The reality is that you can choose to work on a relationship, but *both* people must commit to putting in 100 per cent. Most people I used to know had never picked up a self-development book in their life; they were emotionally unaware and didn't care to do the work. You aren't one of those people – the fact that you are reading this book means you've put yourself in the minority who want to be better and create more. This means that along the way you will need to make hard choices about what you will tolerate. Yes, we get what we tolerate, not what we want. Always choose peace. Peace is the most valuable commodity in my life.

In conclusion of this section, use the power of momentum to propel you forward, and take small actions every day that will compound themselves to create higher interest in your life. Make a plan and try to stick to it, because discipline really creates space for you to be creative and access a flow state. Raise your standards so that you feel energetically in a powerful place. And lastly, take 100 per cent responsibility. The idea that we need to take full responsibility for our lives and how we live them is one of the concepts that made the biggest shift for me personally. So many of us are waiting for someone else to fix things: for the government to change, for the weather to be better, for our partners to raise their game, or for us to give away our power. When we take responsibility we can make the quantum leap, because we are harnessing our own personal power.

Most people don't want to take responsibility for their lives; they want to blame everyone else for their misfortunes and lack of success. We need to stop looking outside ourselves for someone to point the finger at, and start looking inwards for the way to move forward. By harnessing these principles and adding them to the book for creating success, I believe you will start to experience huge breakthroughs and ever bigger results.

The power of your peers

Earlier I gave an example of how people in a supermarket would react if someone ran to the front of the shop and shouted, 'I've made fifty thousand pounds a month', and how this was akin to someone running naked across a football pitch. The reality is that not everyone is going to want to embark on a journey of manifesting their dreams; many people will stay in the field of predictability where the masses reside, and they will have a nice life. When you *decide* that you want more and make an unabashed commitment to going for it, then choosing who you want to be around really matters.

As I've been on this journey of personal development, I've heard some experts on success say, 'Share your goals – say them out loud to everybody, so it keeps you accountable.' But I think there is a danger to this, and that the advice needs to be tweaked. There is 100 per cent power in accountability and stating what you want to achieve, but it needs to be said to the *right* people. What do I mean when I say the *right* people? Look, your parents love you, your friends love you, your siblings love you, but it doesn't mean they'll *get it*. In fact because they love you, they will want to protect you from making a bad decision, even if they are the only ones deeming it a bad decision. It's their opinion, not a fact.

Nobody is able to know your deepest desires or what they truly mean for you, and sadly one of the things we are capable of, as humans, is projecting our fears and insecurities onto others. I'm lucky because my mum is a massive believer in 'Where there's a will there's a way.' As I have embarked on building my businesses, she's been nothing but supportive (and that has been the same for all my siblings as they've started to set up their own businesses), but I know that not all parents are like that. The same goes for partners: if I had a pound for every person I've worked with who's said, 'My partner is concerned' or 'My partner doesn't think my plan's logical', I'd have made millions from that alone.

I'll never forget standing in my living room, telling my husband I wanted to set up a coaching business and that I *knew* this was my path and I'd be able to make it wildly successful. He had witnessed me, from 2014 to 2016, trying to set up multiple business ideas, from importing wedding dresses from China to sell, to creating beard-oil products and even considering buying a cleaning franchise. He was a bricklayer, and he had been a bricklayer working for the council since his late teens. He earned £1,250 a month, with a percentage upgrade each year, and he believed that would be his job until he retired, just like his parents.

When I said, 'I'm going to create ten thousand pounds of business each month', his reaction was, 'You've said this before and it hasn't happened.' I remember something occurring within me when he said that. There was a mixture of frustration and 'Fuck you!', and I was determined to prove him wrong. (I get that from my mum!)

I went on to make that business wildly successful, but it could all have ended in a different way. I could have listened to him, could have believed that what he was saying was right and not have pursued my dream. The reality is that neither of us really knew anybody making that sort of money, so for my husband to comprehend it was too much. It was like trying to speak Spanish to a Chinese person – it just didn't have any meaning.

In order to set up my coaching business, I needed to take 'one more course'. I had to use my husband's credit card to put this scarily huge amount of money (£6,000) on it, as I'd maxed out all of mine while building my products business. I didn't need him to believe in me at that moment, because I believed in myself. It's scary to believe in yourself. We are so trained, as humans, to need validation from others, to need someone else to say they believe in us, but something deep inside me just *knew* it was possible.

Don't get me wrong: it was scary, but I was determined. My husband didn't question my dreams because he didn't believe in me; he questioned me because he loves me and wanted to protect me from making mistakes. He didn't want to see me lose more money or change my mind again.

One year after that conversation, my husband handed in his notice to the council and decided to set up his own bricklaying business. He was inundated with work; it was ridiculous. But since we had decided that we wanted more freedom, and to enable him to walk away from constant manual labour, he took over the online products business and we began to work from home together. And we have been doing that for the last seven years.

If you share your dream with people who don't get it – people who are so stuck in the mainstream way of life, thinking (like the majority) about creating a predictable life – then you cannot expect to be met with a crazy amount of support. It's not their fault. That's why finding communities in which you can share crazy dreams is so important. I joined a programme where conversation about extraordinary success was normal, and if you said, 'I've earned fifty thousand a month', people celebrated you, rather than judging you.

I promise you those spaces exist. I created my memberships for exactly that reason – to create containers where hearing your big-ass goals is safe; where you will be met with support and excitement, not questioning and doubt. Your peers have the power to lift you up, motivate and excite you, or to make you doubt yourself. If your partner doesn't get it now, that's okay. If your parents are questioning, that's okay. Remember: they don't need to get it for you to be a success. This is *your* journey, not theirs! Find your new tribe and cheerleaders and watch how their energy can have a positive impact on you.

19.

*Just f*cking manifest it!*

As we come to the end of our journey in this book, I truly hope you now have more clarity, focus and inspiration to move boldly towards your dreams and towards creating success on your own terms. My intention is that you have some clear-action steps on how to implement the VIA Manifesting Method® (see Part Two) and can feel confident that whatever you desire to shift in your life is *possible*. You are also armed with an understanding of what could be blocking your success and how to overcome it (Part Three), so there are no excuses for staying stuck or for wondering what the heck is going on inside your head.

You officially have all my secrets to manifest your dream life. And now, whenever you desire something, I want you to hear me in your head gently whispering, 'Just f*cking manifest it!'

One of the biggest lessons I want to share with you as a parting gift is the reminder to be fiercely protective of your energy, as it's the most valuable asset you have for creating your life. We have talked a lot about the *inner* game of creating success, and to conclude I'd like to explore how the *external* world affects us and what we can do to protect our energy, because what we allow to come into our lives and seep into our pores will begin to project and create our external world.

Think of a goldfish, a beautiful fish covered in perfect orange scales, bursting with potential and blueprinted for mega-fishy success in the greatest ponds around. Now take that fish and stick it in a bowl of dirty water full of toxins. No matter how many times that fish has been to the gym, downed a green juice and taken supplements, it's going to see the end of its life pretty soon, as the dirty water begins to seep into it. The environment of that fish will eventually poison it. That's why as much as success is an inner game, it's also about making sure that everything on the outside that is coming in is conducive to you getting what you want. It's imperative that you are intentional and conscious about what you are letting into your life, as it is potentially seeping into your pores and affecting your happiness.

If you spend every morning listening to the news, which is informing you of all the disasters that have happened across the world, think of yourself as that fish. Remember that subconscious minds learn through repetition and if, on a daily basis, you're hearing that the world is a horrible place to be in, you can bet your bottom dollar that will be your reality. Think about what you are letting into your life. Is it helping your energy grow or draining your vital life force? You need energy so that you can get shit done! That means you need to actively choose *how* to generate such energy in your life, instead of letting your environment toxify you.

Making sure that you are getting enough fresh air, are immersing yourself in nature and are getting sufficient sunshine on your skin are all *free* things that are proven to help generate energy. The way we can create more energy in our lives is also by choosing to fill them with 'Fuck, yes!' moments (see Chapter 6) that inspire and invigorate us.

What do I mean by a 'Fuck, yes!' moment? I mean anything that brings you joy in life. Think about all the things – big and small – that make you feel good. Then add *more* of them into your life. Here is an example of my 'Fuck, yes!' list that I created at the start of 2023:

- Having a warm coffee with a beautiful view in the morning, before the kids wake up.
- Travelling to three new countries and at least one new city.
- Trying as many plant-based *pastéis de nata* as I can, so that I can find the best one.
- Learning how to sew a dress, so that I can whip up cute outfits for my girls.

- Having a bubbly bath with my hubby, with cocktails in hand, of course.
- Celebrating my tenth wedding anniversary with a fabulous party with our closest friends and family.
- Holding a live event in a really inspiring location, such as the Shard in London.
- Seeing one of my favourite comedians live onstage.

There are little and big things that can fill your cup, make your life meaningful and cause you to smile. The compound effect of these things on a daily, weekly or monthly basis creates a life worth living. For me, there are certain people in my life who, when I spend time with them, leave me feeling as if someone filled my heart with liquid gold. I called them my FMILY – my 'Fuck Me, I Love You' friends (I had one too many Negronis and genuinely thought I was a genius!). FMILY friends *get* you, love to have fun, don't bring drama and genuinely want you to succeed. And you feel the same way about them, too.

There's this horrible misconception that somehow it's lonely at the top. This myth has kept many people stuck, staying small. Who really wants to be seated in a Lamborghini, crying into tissues because they have no one to go on a long drive with? Nobody. So they stay small to avoid this fate, because loneliness is the leading cause of depression. We aren't built to be lonely – we are tribal beings! Having the right people around you is fundamental to having the most successful life you can, and the more I rise, the more I attract incredible humans into my life.

While we can choose to fill our lives with 'Fuck, yes!' moments, note that with the highs there must be lows, for this is life, and life is full of dualities. I took a trip to Mauritius in 2022 and I was lying on the beach gazing up at the sky, which looked like a dramatic picture that had been painted, and it was like I was sitting under two opposing scenes. To my right was the bluest sky that went on for miles, and to my left were the darkest of grey clouds. The divide was so clear, distinct and static, and I was mesmerized by the

The Mastery

contrast – each part being beautiful in its own way. With a few steps one way, I was under the clear blue; and with a few steps the other way, I was under the black cloud. I _was_ in charge because the clouds didn't seem to move for the time we were there.

We always get a choice in life – a choice to bask in the glory of the joys of life or to play the victim and stay in the shadows. When life throws us a dark cloud, we can turn the other way and walk towards the light. It may be a long walk. It may not be an easy walk. But we can always walk to where the sky is blue.

No one can take that away from you: your freedom to walk into the sunlight.

No one has the power to keep you stuck under the rain clouds if you do not want to be there.

You are stronger than you know, wiser than you know and you can get through any shit if you want to. I believe in _you_. Life is about contrast and duality. We need the grey to appreciate the blue. We need the dark to appreciate the light.

So be grateful for it all, learn from it all and you will grow from it all. And I promise that the next time you land in Antarctica, or you get led down dark alleys or are seated under a grey sky, you have the power to choose what you do. This is your _one_ life. I implore you to make it count.

So be crystal-clear on what success really means to you, and start connecting more deeply with yourself, so that you can uncover your unique blueprint.

Curate and lock in a powerful vision for your life. Make sure you declare that it is non-negotiable, and feel that in your body.

Commit to aligning your subconscious scripts with your conscious desires, so that you feel in the flow and are no longer held back by the subconscious mind's primitive safety-and-survival mechanism. You have the power to override that system and to teach your mind new stories that will support you. And if you ever need help with Subconscious Rescripting®, then I have programmes to help you.

Remember to celebrate. Celebrate the small wins, the big

milestones and all the birthdays. Every year you make it another time around the sun is a success.

Don't underestimate the value of each and every breath. Take a moment to give your breath some gratitude daily, because just a few minutes without your breath and your chance of moving forward is gone.

Take relentless, bold action – not because you need to, but because you *want* to. This journey called life is meant to be fun, and the trip to Success-ville should be a blast, not a burden.

And then, in the words of my first book, you've got to 'Just f*cking do it!' Life is too short for playing small, and no one is going to aim for your dreams on your behalf. I wish they could, but they won't.

Use the tools I've given you, and the VIA Manifesting Method®, to make that road trip to Success-ville feel as full of flow and ease as possible. Yes, you may take a wrong turn on the way, or you may need to stop at the services for supplies, but even if there are road-blocks or diversions en route, that's okay. This is your life, and you get the chance to jump back in the driver's seat and start steering the wheel again. Hit a pothole? Take a minute to look for the learning and then keep f*cking going.

You were made for *more*. Never forget that.

You were designed to succeed. Never forget that.

It's all part of your soul journey and your own growth, and it's your responsibility to show the heck up for it! This is the movie of your life: you are the main character and you can dictate how the story goes.

And remember: stop looking for the outside world to validate you – you are a miracle, you are full of potential; you are a f*cking success simply because you are *you*.

Now go and do big things, baby.

Acknowledgements

Writing this book was truly a labour of love and has felt really challenging, given the season of my life.

At the same time as birthing this book, I had just birthed my fourth child and therefore writing this book over the last year – while bringing up little humans, growing my business and also building our dream home – has definitely felt a lot. Not to mention the sleep deprivation! I would never have been able to do it without the support of some incredible humans in my life.

First, the biggest amount of love and gratitude goes to my parents-in-law, Andrea and Kevin. You have been the greatest support with our children, allowing me much-needed space not only to write, but also to get through the arduous editing process. Without you, this book wouldn't have been possible. I love you both and couldn't ask for better grandparents for my children. Thank you from the bottom of my heart.

Thank you to my agent, Jessica Killingley, and to my editor, Jamie Birkett, for helping me get this message to the world; for believing in me enough to let me write another book and for supporting me in crafting a book that will change lives.

In addition I want to send my love and gratitude to all of my readers, fans and followers for the unwavering love and support you have given me over the years. You have become my extended family and have enabled me to create my own version of a successful life, and I really wish the same for you.

Then there's my mother – for always showing me that nothing in life is impossible, for being the role model for resilience and the most creative and resourceful human on this planet that I've ever met. I love you.

Acknowledgements

And last, but by no means least, my husband Richard, for your unwavering support. Without your love and ability to be a super-dad, this book would never exist. I couldn't have created the life we have now without you by my side. I love you with every ounce of my being.